WORLD'S WEIRDEST NEWS STORIES

FROM THE PAGES OF **FORTEAN TIMES**

WORLD'S WEIRDEST NEWS STORIES

FROM THE PAGES OF **FORTEAN TIMES**

COMPILED BY
Paul Sieveking

DESIGN
Etienne Gilfillan

ILLUSTRATIONS
Martin Ross

EDITOR IN CHIEF
David Sutton

PUBLISHING & MARKETING
Russell Blackman
020 7907 6488
russell_blackman@dennis.co.uk

BOOKAZINE MANAGER
Dharmesh Mistry
020 7907 6100
dharmesh_mistry@dennis.co.uk

MAG**BOOK**

WORLD'S WEIRDEST NEWS STORIES is published by Dennis Publishing Ltd, 30 Cleveland Street, London W1T 4JD. Company registered in England. The MagBook brand is a trademark of Dennis Publishing Ltd. All material © Dennis Publishing Ltd, licensed by Felden 2010, and may not be reproduced in any form without the consent of the publishers.
World's Weirdest News ISBN 1-907232-79-6
All material copyright 2010.
Printed at Stones the Printers Limited

LICENSING AND SYNDICATION
To license this product, contact Ornella Roccaletti
020 7907 6134 / ornella_roccaletti@dennis.co.uk
For syndication enquiries, contact Anj Dosaj:
020 7907 6132 / anj_dosaj@dennis.co.uk

DENNIS PUBLISHING LTD
DIGITAL PRODUCTION MANAGER: Nicky Baker
PRODUCTION DIRECTOR: Robin Ryan
MANAGING DIRECTOR OF ADVERTISING:
Julian Lloyd-Evans
NEWSTRADE DIRECTOR: Martin Belson
EXECUTIVE DIRECTOR: Kerin O'Connor

CHIEF OPERATING OFFICER: Brett Reynolds
GROUP FINANCE DIRECTOR: Ian Leggett
CHIEF EXECUTIVE: James Tye
CHAIRMAN: Felix Dennis

HOW TO CONTACT US
MAIL: 30 Cleveland Street, London W1T 4JD
PHONE: 020 7907 6000
EMAIL AND WEB
Website: www.forteantimes.com

To contact advertising:
James Clements 020 7907 6724
james_clements@dennis.co.uk

Change your address, open or renew a subscription or report any problems at www.subsinfo.co.uk
0844 844 0049

WORLD'S WEIRDEST NEWS STORIES

CONTENTS

explore the universe!

TELESCOPES • MOUNTS • ACCESSORIES • BINOCULARS • CAMERAS • NIGHT VISION • SOFTWARE
BOOKS • MICROSCOPES • FILTERS • SOLAR FILTERS & SCOPES • SPOTTING SCOPES • EYEPIECES, ETC.

WORLD'S WEIRDEST NEWS STORIES
FROM THE PAGES OF FORTEAN TIMES

Welcome to this collection of the **WORLD'S WEIRDEST NEWS STORIES** drawn from the pages of **Fortean Times** magazine.

These 500-plus tales of the unexpected, the unlikely and the unbelievable have been gathered over the last 20-odd (sometimes very odd) years from newspapers all around the world. If they teach us anything, it's that our planet is a highly unpredictable place – one in which all sorts of people (not to mention our friends in the animal kingdom) do the strangest things, in which bizarre coincidences occur with remarkable regularity and where a sort of spontaneous surrealism has a way of overtaking the world of the everyday.

So, here are the news stories that don't usually make the headlines. Meet the Indian brothers fined for keeping a pet ghost, the Chinese woman who crashed her car while giving her dog a driving lesson, the French bankrobber who disguised himself as an aubergine and the talking goat with a message from God...

Chapter 1

STRANGE BEHAVIOUR

There's nowt so queer as folk, they say.
From the business man who spent
10 years taking his revenge on a fly
to the fearless granny who fought off a
robber by squeezing his gonads in her
vice-like grip, we'd tend to agree...

ODD OBSESSIONS

WAVE HELLO, SAY GOODBYE

Joseph W Charles, 82, retired in October 1992 from his 'job' as the Waving Man in Berkeley, California. Every day for 30 years, he had stood in his front yard during morning rush hour and waved to motorists. *[AP] 8 Oct 1992.*

PRIEST PUNCHER

Great grandfather Ettore Gagliano, 84, was under psychiatric examination after punching a priest in the Milan Duomo – his 58th (or 158th) clerical victim to date. "I'm quite sane; I have a mission in life," said Sr Gagliano, who liked to ambush his prey from under the cathedral eaves. *Direct Action #79, May 1992; D.Star, 7 June 1993.*

LABOUR OF LOVE

For 10 years, Prof. Hitoshi Kodama has worked on his 1,200-page Japanese-Friesian dictionary. Only two Japanese, including himself, speak Friesian, a dialect in northern Holland. No Friesian-speaking Dutch are known to speak Japanese. "It's a labour of love," he said. *D.Express, 11 Sept 1999.*

GET A LIFE

Les Stewart from Queensland won a place in the *Guinness Book of Records* after completing the World's Longest Typing Marathon. He used up 16 years of his life, seven manual typewriters, 1,000 ink ribbons and 19,990 sheets of paper to type out the numbers one to a million entirely in words. "It helped occupy my time," he said. *Hello! 3 Oct 2000.*

THERE'S MORTAR LIFE

Ronnie Crossland, 59, from Sharlston, West Yorkshire, has spent the last 15 years taking photographs of more than 1,000 cement mixers, which he says "are things of incredible beauty". The retired lorry driver has travelled more than 200,000 miles (322,000km) in search of new mixers. He used to be a trainspotter, but gave it up because it was too boring. *Sun, 25 Sept 2002.*

BACKWARDS TO PEACE

Harpeet Devi, a taxi driver in Bhatinda, India, once had to drive 35 miles (56km) backwards after his gears became stuck in reverse. He liked it so much he decided always to drive that way, and so, for the past two years, he and his passengers have reversed through traffic at up to 25mph (40km/h). He has covered 7,500 miles (12,000km) backwards. He now wants to reverse into Pakistan, taking with him a message of peace and friendship. *Irish Examiner, 24 Dec 2003.*

NO FLY ZONE

Hu Xilin from Zhejiang province in China lost a £13,000 deal 10 years ago after a fly landed on his client's food during a business lunch. He swore revenge, started swatting the insects whenever he could and built special contraptions to trap and kill them. He claims to have killed eight million flies (estimated to weigh 88lb/40kg) and can now identify 25 different species. He plans to recruit a "swat" team of fly-killers at a cost of £20,000. *Ananova, 25 May 2004.*

DOTTY DEVOTION

Pat and Joe Posey from Maryland have "raised" a Cabbage Patch doll, christened Kevin, as their only son for 19 years. The hideous 12in (30cm) doll goes everywhere with them. They talk to him and he "replies" through Joe putting on his voice. Joe and Kevin go on frequent fishing trips together. Kevin has his own playroom, a red doll-sized Chevrolet Corvette car, a pet dog, a full wardrobe and a £2,000 college fund. The Poseys prefer him to their real child, an adult daughter named Vicky. *Sun, 25 Aug 2004.*

CLOVER COLLECTORS

Edward Martin of Alaska claims to have collected "more than 76,000" four-leafed clovers; but he is challenged by George Kaminski, a long-term convict who has collected 72,927 in the grounds of various Pennsylvania prisons. So much for them being lucky, then. *Independent on Sunday, 27 Mar 2005.*

" He went home, severed his testicles and returned to the club with his trophies in a bag "

GOLFING TRIBUTE

Douglas Jones, 57, hurled some 3,000 golf balls into Joshua Tree National Park, California, from his car for more than a year, and left fruit and vegetables along park roads. Rangers spent 370 hours cleaning up, at a cost of $9,000. Jones was finally caught in August and said the balls were to "honour deceased golfers" and the food was for stranded hikers. He was charged with abandoning property and littering. *[AP] 18 Sept 2009.*

NOWT SO QUEER

IDLE HAND

Thomas Passmore of Norfolk, Virginia, cut off his hand because he thought it was possessed by the devil, then refused to let surgeons at Sentara Norfolk General Hospital reattach it. He then sued them for $3 million, saying they should have known he was crazy. *(London) Eve. Standard, 14 May 1996.*

OUT ON A LIMB

Fire-fighters in Trimdon, Co. Durham, rescued Gary Carter, 22, who was found asleep 25ft (7.6m) up a sycamore tree outside the Red Lion pub after an all-day drinking session. He didn't wake up, even when they lowered him to the ground and took him to hospital for a check-up. "It's a mystery how he got there," said publican Alice Hodgson. "It's a bare trunk all the way up with the branches only at the top. But there he was, sound asleep, with his head dangling down like a big leaf. " Carter himself had no idea how he got up the tree. *Guardian, Times, 30 Oct 2001.*

ROOSTER BOOSTER

For a week, a middle-aged couple in Wacken, a village in Schleswig-Holstein, northern Germany, were woken by the deafening crowing of a cockerel. Jens Nagel and his wife called police, who discovered a stereo system in the adjoining flat with its speakers bolted towards the party wall. It had a timing device that played a tape of a crowing cockerel at 100 decibels between 2am and 4am for 20 minutes, with gaps in between. The neighbours had gone away on holiday, having rigged up this sonic instrument of torture. The motive was unclear, as there was no history of animosity. *[R] 15 Feb; Guardian, 17 Feb 2005.*

CAERPHILLY DOES IT

Geoff Huish, 26, was so certain England would win a rugby match he told friends at the Leigh Social Club in Caerphilly, south Wales: "If Wales win I'll cut my balls off." They thought he was joking, but when Wales won 11-9, he went home, severed his testicles and returned to the club wearing a kilt with his trophies in a bag. He was rushed to hospital with severe blood loss and there was talk of fitting him with a prosthetic scrotum. *D.Mirror, Sun, 8 Feb 2005.*

VENGEANCE SWIPES CAKE

A large bearded man crashed a children's party in the Chicago suburb of Oak Forest. When the householder asked him who he was, the 6ft (1.8m) tall, 275lb (125kg) intruder replied: "I am vengeance. I am the knight. I am Batman." He then went into the kitchen and ate a piece of birthday cake before driving off in a red 1988 Cadillac. *Chicago Sun-Times, 30 Aug 2005.*

FISH ASSAULT

Alan Bennie, 20, was walking through Zetland Park in Grangemouth, Stirlingshire, at 8.30pm one evening in May 2005 when he was accosted by David Evans, 22, carrying a large fish. "Do you want to kiss my fish?" he asked. Bennie made no reply and walked on. "You answer me next time I ask you to kiss a fish," said Evans, and slapped him round the face with the fish.

Bennie encountered some policemen, who asked him why he had fish guts and scales sticking to his face, after which they arrested Evans. He was later jailed for six months. *Edinburgh Eve. News, 22 Nov 2005.*

CRUEL RELIEF

A Japanese nurse who tried to relieve her work stress by tearing off patients' nails was jailed for three years and eight months. The 32-year-old, who worked at a hospital in Kyoto, tore off the fingernails and toenails of six female patients immobilised by strokes or other illnesses. *Surrey Leader, 24 Jan 2006.*

DUNG HAZARD

A couple in Modesto, California, were arrested after officials discovered a miniature horse living in their kitchen and dining room. They were charged with child endangerment as the woman's son was forced to sleep in a tent inside his bedroom to protect himself from the flies attracted by the mounds of horse dung, of which there was a large quantity. *Irish Independent, 21 July 2007.*

EYEBROW ATROCITY

A 25-year-old man was waiting to meet a friend on a street corner in Hong Kong's Shek Kip Mei district at 1.30am on 17 September 2007 when a black car pulled up and three men jumped out and grabbed him. They beat him unconscious and when he woke up on a hillside hours later, he found his eyebrows had been shaved off and he had lost HK$300. *Bangkok Post, 18 Sept 2007.*

MOO-VE ALONG

Michelle Allen, 32, was arrested in Middletown, Ohio, after chasing her children down the road dressed in a cow costume, before urinating on a neighbour's front porch. She was told to go home, but was later found blocking a road and was rearrested. She then appeared in court, still dressed as a cow. *(Dublin) Metro, 1 Oct 2008.*

FUNNY OLD WORLD

PECKED BY PENGUINS

Nimrod Nbini, 76, charged with stabbing and beating a penguin to death, told a Cape Town magistrate that he acted in self-defence after being pecked. *(Brisbane) Courier-Mail, 31 Mar 1992.*

STICK WITH IT

Dutchman Wim Alaerds, 24, had more than doubled the world pole-sitting record by the time he left his 8ft (2.4m) perch on 21 June 1997 after 51 days. The annual pole-sitting championship began at Soltau, near Hamburg, on 1 May. *[AP] 23 June 1997.*

NO REST FOR THE WICKED

A Swedish nurse who had a different husband for every day of the week was jailed for a year in Stockholm for bigamy. Suzanna Borg, 30, found the men through dating agencies and convinced all seven she had to do shift work for the other six days. She managed to maintain the deception for a whole year. *D.Mail, 4 April 1998.*

MIGHT NEVER HAPPEN

Lloyd Albright, a computer programmer at the Kennedy Space Center, hid in a cave in southeast Ohio for two days to avoid a meteor he thought was going to hit the Atlantic and cause a tidal wave 200ft (60m) high. Police found him with camping equipment, dried food and 16 guns. *[AP] 19 Aug 1999.*

BITING FRENZY

A 13-month-old boy was bitten 30 times by a group of more 13 other babies at a nursery in Lovran, Croatia, after the class nanny stepped out of the room to change another baby's nappy. Frane Simic was covered in a series of deep bite wounds all over his body, including his face.

Dr Sime Vuckov, head of the hospital in Rijeka which treated the boy, had never seen anything like it. The nanny was charged with negligence. *Sky News, 23+27 Oct 2003.*

THEY SCORE! HE SHOOTS!

Scores were still level shortly before the end of a Chilean amateur football match. Then Bandera striker El Rulo scored the winner. His joy was short-lived as an opposition player pulled a revolver out of his shorts and shot him three times. Two shots missed, but the third hit El Rulo's shoulder. He was taken to hospital, while the shooter went on the run. *Irish Times, 26 Jan 2004.*

CAN-DO SPIRIT

A patrol was watching the approaches to Niagara Falls on 27 July when along the upper rapids came a man and his dog in a strange vessel propelled by a shovel. It comprised an inner tube, child's inflatable dinghy, car luggage rack "for stability" and a rug, all held together with string. Man and dog were lifted to safety. A police spokesman commented: "Ignorance of the local waterway, and drugs, were a factor." *Independent on Sunday, 1 Aug 2004.*

GOATCHA!

A 93-year-old woman who claimed to have a grip "like iron" after years of milking goats fought off two robbers by grabbing one of them by the testicles and squeezing hard. "He started screaming like an animal," said Soja Popova, from Klaipeda, Lithuania. The man's yelps alerted neighbours, who called police. *(London) Eve. Standard, 18 Aug 2005.*

" The opposing player pulled a revolver out of his shorts and shot him three times "

ARMLESS FUN

Colin Smith was stopped by police on State Highway 29 near Tauranga in New Zealand on 23 March after driving at 75mph (120km/h) in a 60mph zone while steering with one foot and operating the pedals with the other. The 32-year-old unemployed man, who had several passengers, said he was born with no arms, had never had a licence, and had been driving this way for years with no problems. He was fined £60 and barred from driving. *The Press (Christchurch, NZ), D.Telegraph, 25 Mar 2006.*

JUST SHUT UP

A desperate housewife called police in Speyer, Germany, after a friend chatted to her for 30 hours non-stop. Ingrid Schuettler, 48, told police she'd invited her friend round for a cup of tea and a chat; but once they started talking, her pal "would not shut up" and continued through the night and the next day. Officers persuaded the friend to leave. *North West Eve. Mail, 10 July 2008.*

NOT HER AGAIN

Hee Orama, 34, a woman in Clarksville, Tennessee, who kept calling 911 to complain that a man refused to marry her, was arrested. The previous week, her incessant 911 'emergencies' were that she couldn't find her car. *New York Post, 9 Nov 2009.*

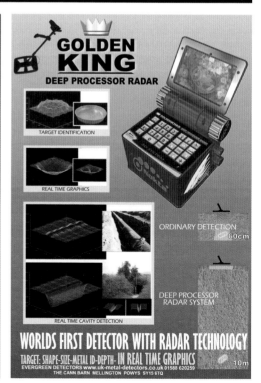

Chapter 2

ANIMAL ANTICS

Just like humans, animals can perform
acts of altruism: dolphins rescuing
swimmers, bears looking after babies.
But what with cat-bothering monkeys,
gatecrashing camels, Nazi raccoons
and murderous squirrels...
who said they were all cuddly?

" A cat called Chiquita adopted a bird that hurt itself when it fell out of its nest "

ANIMAL SAVIOURS

DOLPHIN RESCUE

According to Bangladesh fisheries minister Abdullah al Noman, a baby was swept away from the coastal village of Chakorta during the cyclone on 30 April 1991, which officially claimed at least 125,000 lives. He had been given up for dead when rescuers spotted a dolphin holding him in its mouth to keep him clear of the water. The dolphin allowed villagers to prise the boy from its jaws. He was later treated for leg injuries caused by the dolphin's grip. *[AP] 12 May 1991.*

GORILLA WAR

Shortly before midnight, a troupe of about 60 gorillas entered the village of Olamze in Cameroon, near the border with Equatorial Guinea, looking for a young gorilla captured earlier in the day by local hunter Ntsama Ondo. The villagers fired guns to scare them away, but they returned the next night and beat on the doors and windows. The village chief ordered Ondo to release his captive. According to the Cameroon news-paper *L'Action*: "The assailants returned to the forest with shouts of joy, savouring their victory." *[AFP] 23 Oct 1997.*

CARE BEAR

A mother bear appears to have cared for a missing 16-month-old Iranian toddler who was found safe and sound three days later in the animal's den, the *Kayhan* newspaper reported. The child's parents, nomads in western Lorestan province, returned to their tent after working in the fields to find him missing. Three days later, a search party found the baby, who they said had probably been breast-fed by a mother bear, in a den six miles (10km) away from the nomadic settlement. He was in good health. *[R] 2 Oct 2001.*

COW RESCUE

Farmer Kim Riley, 43, was swept off her feet by the current as she tried to turn a group of cows away from the flooded Manawatu River at her farm in Woodville, New Zealand, in early morning darkness. She grabbed a cow marked number 569, which struggled to the bank. Riley lost 15 of the 350 cows that were swept into the river. She said the animal that saved her, "an ugly old tart", would get a bit of extra attention from now on. *[AP] 17 Feb 2004.*

PACHYDERM FIRST AID

A herd of elephants blockaded a railway track in Dooars Forest in eastern India to protect a male hit by a goods train. Several trains had to be halted while vets treated the injured animal. *[AFP] 19 Mar 2004.*

CANNY CAT

A cat called Chiquita adopted a bird that hurt itself when it fell out of its nest in Porto Alegre, Brazil, and cannot fly. They ate from the same plate. Chiquita's owner, Nair de Souiza, named the bird Pitico. Souza said: "Pitico has even started to eat meat, because the two of them only eat together. But Chiquita uses Pitico to help her catch other birds. It is really unbelievable!" *The Press (Christchurch, NZ), 4 Feb 2006.*

RESCUED BY DOGS

Hundreds of people flocked to the village of Narhan in the eastern Indian state of Bihar to see a baby girl who was saved by three stray dogs after she was abandoned by her mother in an orchard under a mound of mud and leaves. "The dogs removed the soil and began to bark and the baby started crying, which drew the attention of the villagers," said a government official. He added that the girl had been adopted by a childless couple. *Independent, (Dublin) Herald AM, 23 April 2008.*

URSINE CHARITY

Azra Noonari, 39, was at Woburn Safari Park in Bedfordshire with her two young children when a bear took a hubcap off the car that had stopped in front of her, and then walk towards her car. "It put the hubcap down and then banged on the window, as if it was trying to get my attention," she said. "It was almost like it wanted to give me the hubcap." The hubcaps on her car had been stolen at her home in Luton a few weeks earlier. *Metro, 21 Aug 2008.*

BEASTLY FEASTS

A JONAH MOMENT

A hamster survived being eaten by a hunting dog. A five-year-old girl heard her pet, called Pravda, squeaking inside the dog so vets opened up its stomach. Pravda, who weighed only 150g (just over 5oz), was unconscious, but made a full recovery after the vet massaged its heart. The 10-month-old dog, called Malysch, also recovered after the operation. *D.Express, Metro, 17 Nov 2000.*

CARNIVOROUS COW

Farmers in a Serbian village were surprised to find that it was not a fox that had eaten 12 chickens, but a neighbour's cow. Radisa Dinic told the newspaper *Glas Javosti*: "The only way I can see to stop my cow eating any more of my neighbours' chickens is to share my own meat dinners with her." *Ananova, 4 July 2002.*

HUNTER BECOMES PREY

A golden eagle made a meal of a dachshund taking part in a rabbit

hunt in Halland, south-western Sweden, on 8 January. One consolation
for Valdemar Nilsson, the dog's owner, was that under Swedish law, the
government compensates losses of cattle and dogs caused by
protected species such as bears, wolves, wolverines, lynx and eagles.
[R] 9 Jan 2003.

FLESH-EATING BUNNIES

Robben Island, where Nelson Mandela was jailed for 27 years, has
become home to hundreds of carnivorous rabbits that are killing and
eating nesting birds. A wildlife expert said they moved around "like
packs of rats". *Nottingham Eve. Post, 12 April 2006.*

GATECRASHING CAMEL

Staff at the Mullingar Equestrian Centre in central Ireland had to
postpone their Christmas party after Gus the camel chomped his way
through 200 mince pies, 150 sandwiches and seven cans of Guinness
while staff were getting changed. The 11-year-old camel, originally from
Morocco, cracked open the cans with his teeth after the door to his stall
was left open. *[R] 6 Dec; Independent, 9 Dec 2006.*

BEASTS BEHAVING BADLY

MILLIPEDES STOP TRAIN

A train was brought to a halt in the mountains of western Japan near
Osaka by a swarm of millipedes, up to 6cm (2.4in) long, which covered
a 400 metre (1,312ft) shadowy upward stretch of track. The single-car-
riage train, carrying only two passengers, skidded to a halt after crush-
ing enormous numbers of the white creatures. *[AFP] 12 Oct 2003.*

NAZI RACCOONS

In 1934, Goering released a pair of raccoons into the woods near Kassel
"to enrich the Reich's fauna". Today, Germany is overrun with more than
a million of the 2ft (60cm) North American creatures, which have no
natural predators, rifle through rubbish bins, steal food from houses and

endanger local wildlife. They are spreading to France, Belgium, Holland and Denmark. *Sun, 10 Mar; Independent on Sunday, 14 Mar 2004.*

HOT CROSS BUNNY

Groundsmen at Devizes Cricket Club in Wiltshire were startled when they lit a paraffin-soaked bonfire and a rabbit shot out with its tail ablaze. They didn't see where it went, but 30 minutes later their nearby shed, containing mowers, wheelbarrows, and other implements, went up in flames, causing £60,000 worth of damage. There was no sign of the rabbit's remains, suggesting it might have got away. *Times, Guardian, BBC News, 13 Aug 2004.*

MURDEROUS SQUIRRELS

A gang of bloodthirsty black squirrels attacked and killed a large stray dog that was barking at them in a park in Lazo, a village in the Maritime Territory of Russia's far east. Three local men were too late to stop the attack, which lasted about a minute. "[The squirrels] literally gutted the dog," said a local journalist. "When they saw the men, they scattered in different directions, taking pieces of their kill away with them." A villager suggested a pine cone shortage had led the squirrels to seek other food sources, but scientists were sceptical. *BBC News, 1 Dec; Scotsman, 3 Dec 2005.*

FISH STARTS FIRE

Kipper, an 8in (20cm) catfish, is thought to have triggered a fire in Poole, Dorset, when it fought with a rival in their tank on 7 May. Water splashed out of the aquarium and landed on an electric plug below, sending a power surge up the tank's light cable. This burnt the plastic lid, which melted and dripped onto a leather sofa, which caught alight. The blaze soon engulfed the lounge and set off an alarm. The four occupants were treated for smoke inhalation. All six fish in the tank perished. *Sun, D.Mail, 9 May 2006.*

MONKEY BUSINESS

A man in Zhengzhou, Henan province, China, read in a local paper that monkeys in Zhengzhou Zoo had mistreated cats placed on their hill to eliminate mice. Incensed, he stood in front of the monkey hill holding up a sign censuring the zoo's management. A monkey grabbed the sign and ripped it to pieces. *Morning Star, 13 Mar 2007.*

TERRIBLE TUSKERS

An elephant in Orissa, eastern India, has turned highway robber. It blocks traffic and refuses to let vehicles pass unless drivers give it food. Police have received a barrage of complaints from terrified motorists. Meanwhile in the Bishnupur district of Bengal, an elephant herd passed through villages foraging for ripe fruit – and unearthed as many as seven recently dug graves. *Metro, Guardian, 29 May; (Dublin) Metro, 22 June 2007.*

WORMS OF DESTRUCTION

An invasion of unidentified worms – 2cm long, thorny green with black stripes – has forced 50 herdsmen and their families from their grassland homes in Usu, in northwest China's Xinjiang region, taking 20,000 head of livestock with them. The worms are packed up to 3,000 per square metre and chew through the grasslands like lawnmowers, leaving only brown soil in their wake. Xinjiang has in the past used chickens and ducks to fight locusts, but they have shown little interest in the pesky worms. *[R] 8 May 2009.*

A DOG'S LIFE

LUCKY DOG

A 10-month-old mixed breed dog named Dosha was hit by a car in Clearwater, California, on 15 April 2003. Then a policeman shot her in the head to put her out of her misery. Finally, she was put in an animal centre freezer to await disposal. Two hours later, she was found standing upright in a body bag and is recovering well. Her injured muzzle from the accident was minor compared to hypothermia and a bullet in the head. *[AP,R] 23 April 2003.*

DOGGONE

Dogs in Australia's Northern Territory are getting high by licking toxins from the backs of cane toads (an introduced species killing off local fauna). Veterinarian Megan Pickering in Katherine, three hours' drive south of Darwin, said some dogs were becoming addicted to the hallucinogens; she had treated more than 30 dogs that had overdosed on bufo toxin. *Brisbane Courier-Mail, 18 Feb; Adelaide Advertiser, 19 Feb 2005.*

"BEST CAT" DOG

It was probably the first time a dog's memorial service was attended by 300 cats. A schnauzer-Siberian husky mix named Ginny was eulogised on 19 November 2005 at the Westchester Cat Show in White Plains, NY. Ginny was named Cat of the Year in 1998 for her uncanny skill and bravery in finding and rescuing endangered tabbies on Long Island's South Shore. She once threw herself against a vertical pipe at a construction site to topple it and reveal kittens trapped inside. Another time, she ignored the cuts on her paws as she dug through a box of broken glass to find an injured cat. She died in August aged 17. *[AP] 10 Nov 2005.*

CANINE LEFTIE

Sandy, a three-year-old Shetland sheepdog rescued from an animal shelter by Barbara and Danny Willcock of Manchester, refuses to turn right. At best, she sits down and won't budge; at worst, she runs away. The Willcocks would like to take Sandy for a stroll in nearby Heaton Park, but that would involve a right turn, so they have to turn left and walk for three miles (4.8km) to reach the park – or drive there. *Guardian, 22 Oct 2005.*

HEIMLICH HOUND

Debbie Parkhurst, 45, was eating an apple at home in Calvert, Maryland, when a piece became lodged in her throat and she began to choke. She lent over a chair and pounded on her chest but could not move the piece. Her two-year-old golden retriever Toby then knocked her to the ground and jumped on her chest repeatedly, dislodging the apple, and licked her face so she would not pass out. She was convinced Toby was not playing and was trying to perform his own version of the Heimlich manoeuvre. *BBC News, 28 Mar; Metro, 29 Mar 2007.*

" Dogs in Australia are getting high by licking toxins off the backs of cane toads "

LAST RITES

SHARK SEND-OFF

The Fijian president, Ratu Sir Penaia Ganilau, was said to be a direct descendant of the shark god Dakuwaqa, so it was entirely fitting that a school of sharks appeared suddenly in Suva harbour on 29 December 1993 to accompany his funeral flotilla out to sea. Sightings even of a single shark in the harbour are rare. *Independent, 31 Dec 1993.*

BEES PAY RESPECTS

Margaret Bell, who kept bees in Leintwardine about 7 miles (11km) from her home in Ludlow, Wales, died in June 1994. Soon after her funeral in Ludlow, mourners saw a swarm of hundreds of bees settle on the corner of Bell Lane, directly opposite 42 Mill Street where Mrs Bell had lived for the last 26 years. They stayed for about an hour before buzzing off over the rooftops. Country lore says you should tell bees of a death so that they can come and say goodbye. *South Shropshire Journal, 24 June [R] 8 Sept 1994.*

CANINE SUICIDE

Shopkeeper Giovanni Cera, 59, was killed when his car was hit by a train at a level crossing near Rome. His Alsatian escaped and ran away. The next day he returned to the scene of the accident and lay down in the road until he was run over and killed by a car. *(London) Eve. Standard, 10 Sept 1999.*

FISH FROM THE GRAVE

Spencer Maffey of Little Hulton, Greater Manchester, found a goldfish floating lifelessly in its tank. Knowing that step-daughter Shauni Riley would want to help bury her pet fish, he put it in the freezer in a tissue paper shroud for four hours until she came home, when they buried it in the garden. Five days later, the family cat came into the kitchen with the wriggling goldfish in his mouth. It was returned to its tank and seemed none the worse for the ordeal. *Manchester Eve. News, 14 July 2000.*

SNIFFER CAT RUBBED OUT

A very effective "sniffer cat" employed by Russian customs was run over and killed in a suspected contract killing. After wandering into a customs checkpoint near Stepnovsky as a stray Siamese kitten last year, Rusik became the scourge of the Stavropol region's mafia by hunting out caviar being smuggled from the Caspian Sea to Moscow. He was mown down by a car in which he had once discovered smuggled sturgeon. Another cat, Barsik, succumbed a few weeks earlier after eating a poisoned mouse. *[AP] 13 July; Irish Times, Guardian, 14 July 2003.*

FRIENDS TILL THE END

A pet dog missed the family's cat so much that he dug up his grave and brought the body back into the house. His owners, Robert and Mavis Bell of Wigan, Greater Manchester, woke to find Oscar, an 18-month-old Lancashire heeler, curled up beside 17-year-old Arthur, the late cat, in his basket. "Arthur's coat was gleaming white," said Mr Bell, 73. "Oscar had obviously licked him clean." Oscar now has a new playmate, a kitten called Limpet. *Times, 10 Jan 2008.*

Chapter 3

THE SPIRIT WORLD

A bottom-slapping poltergeist,
a shadowy figure haunting Sunderland's
football training ground, a bald spook
on the number 903 bus and a burglar
who claims he was held captive
for three days by a ghost!

PESKY POLTS

RAINING STONES

Between 8pm and 10pm on 20 February 1995, stones fell on roofs in Sarulesti, Romania, and a farmer's wife miscarried out of fear. The stone shower resumed the following evening. Although some windows were hit, none was broken. Three policemen investigated, but failed to scare off the invisible stone-thrower, even by firing in the air. *Zig-Zag (Romania), 9 Mar 1995.*

POLTS & VOLTS

Southern Electricity faced a claim that a poltergeist was responsible for Sharon McGrath's £900 electricity bill. It had allegedly turned on lights and equipment, as well as shredding telephone directories and bills at her house in Cowes, Isle of Wight. *Edinburgh Eve. News, 31 Oct 1995.*

POLTER-GOOSED

An Indian woman in Nishan, 125 miles (200km) from Mumbai, was taken to hospital in shock claiming that a poltergeist slapped her on the bottom as she was about to urinate in a public lavatory. The resulting scare was so great that armed guards were posted outside the convenience. Reporters suggested that the polt story was connected to the sale of a plot of land nearby, which was held up because of the public lavatory. *Hong Kong Standard, 5 July 1997.*

ESSEX POLT

A couple fled their council flat in Warley, Essex, claiming a poltergeist had attacked them. Angeline Mussett, 19, said something grabbed her wrist, leaving two scratches, and gave her husband David an electric shock. Baby Joshua moved across a room and was found holding a lost TV remote control at just a few weeks old. The couple think the previous tenant died in the flat. They moved in with relatives while waiting to be rehoused. *Metro, Sun, 31 Aug 2006.*

VILLAGE DISTURBANCE

Families living in the Romanian village of Lilieci claimed evil spirits were breaking windows, sending bicycles flying through the air, moving objects on tables and blowing out candles when there was no wind. The police laughed at them – until they experienced the phenomena first-hand. "There were bottles and things flying around," said a police-man. "I didn't know what to dodge first." A report was filed blaming ghosts and a priest was called in to perform exorcisms. *North West Eve. Mail, 3 Mar 2008.*

TROUBLE WITH DJINN

A Saudi family has taken a djinni (genie) to court, accusing it of leav-ing threatening voicemail, stealing their mobile phones and throwing stones at them. They had moved out of the house near the city of Medina where they had lived for 15 years. A local Sharia court was investigating. Trouble began in 2007. "We began hearing strange noises," said the head of the family. "The children got particularly scared when the djinn started throwing stones. A woman spoke to me first, and then a man. They said we should get out of the house." Djinn are often said to be motivated by revenge or jealousy. *BBC News, 11 July 2009.*

PHANTOM FIGURES

SPOOK UP TOP

The ghost of a bald man, looking at the driver in his mirror, was seen on the top deck of the No 903 coach between Kilmarnock and Ardrossan in Scotland. "Three different drivers have witnessed this," said Mark Fraser, spokesman for Haunted Scotland. "One asked the controller to look though the mirror system and he saw it. The control-ler went upstairs and found no one, but the driver could still see him sitting in the seat." *(Scottish) Sunday Mail, 18 Oct 1998.*

" Coaching staff spotted a shadowy black figure at the team's training ground "

PHANTOM ACROBATS

Drivers passing through Horan Valley outside Haditha, an Iraqi town 220km (140 miles) northeast of Baghdad, have reported "ghosts appearing next to the bridge, naked and doing some acrobatic moves", according to the state-run Alwan weekly. The ghosts were "throwing themselves before cars, causing the drivers to panic". They were so life-like that one motorist thought he had hit a person and reported the accident to the police, who found no sign of a body. *National Post (Toronto), 23 Aug 1999.*

SUFI APPARITION

On 28 March, an apparition of bearded men was said to have appeared on the dome of an 800-year-old shrine to Sufi saint Khwaja Moinuddin Chisti in Ajmer, Rajasthan, northern India. Syed Irfan Usmani, a shrine worker, said one of the figures appeared to be Khwaja himself. In the following three days, about 50,000 pilgrims thronged to the shrine. *Irish Independent, Western Mail, 30 Mar 2002.*

SYRIAN ENTITY

According to the Syrian newspaper *Teshreen*, seven workers had seen "a strange creature", red in colour with a "peasantish" look, in an olive grove near Al-Naiisia in Central Syria. It "remained seated for a while before taking running strides to climb up a tree." Finally, it "rushed skyward with incredible swiftness after leaving a wake of smoky white bubbles." The authorities examined the site, but nothing abnormal was found. *Infobae.com 6 Jun 2004.*

EXPLORER'S GHOST

In a video made to support restoration of the Antarctic huts of Sir Ernest Shackleton and Robert Falcon Scott, Sir Edmund Hillary, 86, the conqueror of Mount Everest, said: "I remember when I first went to Shackleton's hut [at Cape Royds, Ross Island], I distinctly saw Shackleton walking towards me and welcoming me and then it all flashed away and he was gone." Shackleton died in 1922 and is buried on the island of South Georgia. *D.Telegraph (Sydney), 19 Jan; National Post (Toronto), 20 Jan 2005.*

SOCCER SPOOK

Sunderland soccer team won eight games in a row, but their luck changed after coaching staff spotted a shadowy black figure at their training ground in Whitburn, South Tyneside. Two physios chased the apparition before it vanished and striker Stephen Elliott also claims to have seen the ghost – thought (why, heaven knows) to be that of a local recluse and wrecker in the 18th century called Spottee. Shortly after the sightings, the Championship leaders lost 2–1 at home to Reading on 9 April. *D.Mirror, Sun, 16 April 2005.*

GHOSTLY GOINGS-ON

HAUNTED ROAD

In just one year, 26 cars have crashed on the same 500 metre (1,640ft) stretch of the A465 in Stoke Lacy, Herefordshire – the scene of a fatal smash 60 years ago. Drivers said it felt as if the wheel was snatched from their hands. The parish council had called in local ghost-busting minister Kevin Crouch to see if he could exorcise the road. *Sun, 26 Oct 2002.*

GHOST CLOSES INSTITUTE

Students of the Indian Statistical Institute in New Delhi claimed a ghost had knocked on doors, jostled them on staircases and left traces of aftershave and cigarette smoke. They linked the aftershave aroma to a first-year student who had died a month earlier of a rare heart condition. "A fear psychosis gripped some students," said Rajeev Karandikar, head of the prestigious Institute. "We thought it best to allow them to go home if they wanted to." The Institute was temporarily closed. *[R] 21 Sept 2004.*

PHANTOM OF THE LIBRARY

During the evening of 18 January, several students in Texas Southern University's law library heard a voice calling "Hey!" or "Help!" from inside the walls or ceiling. They called the police, who also heard the voice. Firefighters ripped out ceiling tiles and crawled through ductwork in a number of rooms, but couldn't find anyone or anything. *ABC13 Eyewitness News (Houston TX), 19 Jan 2005.*

SPECTRAL ODOUR

A priest was called to a nursing home in Porsgrunn, southern Norway, to deal with a haunting. According to night nurses, the ghost was a previous head nurse, who filled the corridors with the scent of the eau de cologne she used in life: the classic 4711. They were too frightened to work late hours. Sigrid Øyen, head of the nursing home, said things had improved after the priest's blessing. *Expressen (Sweden), 29 Oct 2006.*

BURGLAR HAUNTED

A 36-year-old Malaysian man who broke into a house claims he was held captive by a "supernatural figure" for three days without food and water. The house's owners found him fatigued and dehydrated when they returned from holiday on 11 December, and called an ambulance to take him to hospital. The man told police in Kuala Lumpur that every time he tried to escape, the ghost-like entity shoved him to the ground. *[AP] 14 Dec 2008.*

Chapter 4

MEDICAL MARVELS

Meet the Indian man who blows up balloons with his ears, the Romanian woman who didn't sleep for eight years, the Turkish housewife who gave birth to six sets of triplets, and the metal-eating Peruvian construction worker.

LIVING WONDERS

EMBEDDED CHOPSTICK

Car park attendant Ng Keng Choon, 30, went to a hospital in the northern Malaysian city of Ipoh to be treated for an infection that left him unable to move his right eye. Doctors found a 6cm (2.4in) piece of wooden chopstick running from under his right eye through his nose and to the back of his left eye. It had probably been embedded during an assault five years earlier. He had suffered from impaired vision but had been unaware of the foreign object. He was lucky to be alive, as the chopstick had been nudging against his brain. *[DPA] Sydney Morning Herald, 19 Nov 2003.*

SLEEPLESS

Maria Stelica, 54, from Budeasa in Romania, developed insomnia after her mother died in 1995. "At first I couldn't sleep even though I tried because I was frightened I would dream about my mother, but after a while I did not need it anymore, and not even sleeping pills can put me to sleep now," she said eight years later. Doctors, who have run clinical tests, confirmed her story appeared genuine but could offer no medical explanation for her condition. *Ananova, 8 Dec 2003.*

TRIPLET CHAMPIONS

Last November, Fatma Saygi, 28, who lives in Katha near the Turkish city of Adana, was about to give birth to her sixth set of triplets. Her husband Mehmet earns about £12 a week as a wedding singer. She is not thought to have taken fertility drugs. Eight of her children from previous pregnancies are said to have survived. The record holder is an Italian woman, Madalene Granata, who bore 15 sets of triplets between 1839 and 1886. *Guardian, 6 Nov 2003.*

MYSTERY RASH

Nineteen fifth-graders from Brooklyn, New York, were rushed to hospital on 23 April 2004 after breaking out in a baffling rash. The "hysterical" children from PS177 in Bensonhurst complained of respiratory problems

and skin irritations that some said looked like "a slap in the face".
New York Post, 24 April 2004.

BITING THE BULLET

Wendell Coleman, 47, of Jacksonville, Florida, woke up with a terrible headache on 20 June and checked himself into hospital. A doctor noted he had trouble speaking and his lips appeared badly swollen and marked with powder burns. A bullet was found embedded in his tongue. Coleman didn't realise he had been shot. He said he had been talking to a couple in a parked car the night before when a man pulled out a gun and pressed it against his mouth. He heard the gun fire, but then went home to bed. *D.Express, 24 June; Canberra Times, 25 June 2005.*

NAIL BY MOUTH

Guy Hart, 84, from Placerville, California, coughed up a nail that had been in his body for almost 36 years. The inch-long (2.5cm) spike was fired into his neck by his rotary lawnmower in 1970. Doctors found it nestled inside his ribcage, but decided it was safe to leave it there. A recent X-ray showed it had moved to his lung and he was set to have surgery, but after a coughing fit the nail emerged. *News10 ABC, 15 Feb; Sun, 20 Feb 2006.*

GOING IN SEINE

French doctors have identified a psychological condition, "Paris Syndrome", in which tourists (mostly Japanese) with excessively romantic notions about the French capital go into shock after encountering the reality of unfriendly locals, litter and street crime. A third of victims suffer psychoses. At least four Japanese have had to be repatriated this year, including two women who thought their hotel room was bugged, and a man convinced he was Louis XIV. *Metro, Independent, 23 Oct 2006.*

WOUND TRANSFERRED

Further to the curiosity of a child who inherited his father's birthmark, a woman from St Albans wrote to Dr James Lefanu to tell of a friend who, when pregnant, decided to pierce her ears with a red-hot needle and cork. "Piercing the first ear was so painful, she decided not to proceed

" Xu Pinghui has laughed non-stop for 12 years since suffering a fever at eight months old "

to the second," she wrote. "When her son was born, he had a small hole in his earlobe." *Sunday Telegraph, 4 Mar 2007.*

AN EAR FOR TRICKS

Zhang Xinquan (or Yinming) from Dalian in China's Shandong province can drink water or milk through his nose and then squirt it up to two metres with his eyeballs. He took less than a minute to put out 26 candles in this way. He also uses his ears to blow up two balloons at the same time, a wild talent shared by Sanjay Sharma, 34, in Delhi, who had achieved fame across India. *Morning Star, 19 May; The Australian, 30 April 2007; Toronto Globe & Mail, 29 May 2008.*

GRIN AND CAN'T BEAR IT

The famous "perma-smile" required by the service sector in Japan is driving hundreds of thousands of women mad, according to Makoto Natsume, a leading psychiatrist at Osaka University. Real emotions are being dangerously suppressed by the "smile masks" and depression and mental illness are spreading fast. Many complain of painful muscle and headaches akin to repetitive strain injury. *Irish Independent, 9 Feb 2008.*

ALL HIS FAULT

A 10-year-old boy with obsessive compulsive disorder thought the 9/11 attacks on the World Trade Center were his fault because he failed to step on a particular white mark in the road that day. Experts from University College London, writing in the journal *Neurocase*, claimed he was the first patient to feel responsible for terrorism. *D.Telegraph, 28 June 2008.*

LEGEND CONFIRMED

Yes, Hitler really did have only one ball as the popular wartime song proclaimed. In the 1960s, German army medic Johan Jambor told a priest, Franciszek Pawlar, that the misanthropic corporal sustained abdominal injuries and the loss of a testicle at the battle of the Somme. Herr Jambor felt guilty for having saved Hitler's life. The revelation was only made public 23 years after Jambor died. *D.Express, 20 Nov; Independent, 22 Nov 2008.*

LIFE'S A LAUGH

Xu Pinghui, 13, had laughed non-stop for 12 years since suffering a fever at eight months old. She could not talk so she communicated with different kinds of chuckle. "There is no happiness for us," said her father, Xu Weiming. "Seeing her laughing we feel even sadder than if she were crying." Doctors in Chongqing, central China, planned to carry out a CAT scan in the hope of finding a cure. *Sun, 16 Jan 2009.*

CHAMPION BITE

Police in Chongqing, China, solved a spate of mystery burglaries after finding the culprit was biting his way through steel window bars. Xiong, 23, confessed after a man told detectives he was sharing a hotel room with someone who could crack walnuts with his teeth. Xiong could chew open steel bars up to one centimetre thick. *Sunday Mercury, 14 June 2009.*

METAL MUNCHERS

Margaret Daalmans, 52, an estate agents' secretary from Rotterdam, Netherlands, complained of stomach pains. An X-ray revealed 78 forks and teaspoons. These were removed and she made a full recovery. Doctors in Cajamarca city, Peru, removed 24oz (680g) of metal from the stomach of construction worker Requelme Abanto, 26, including nails, coins, rusted copper wire and scrap metal. He ate the metal for months; "I swallowed 17 nails in February and didn't die," he said. "Five-inch nails, all in one day." He told a TV channel that he might now do it in public "as sport". *Metro, Sun, 29 Oct; [AP] 12 Nov 2009.*

HUMAN ANOMALIES

BORN BITING

Sean Keany was born in Basingstoke hospital with 12 teeth. His mother Sarah, 21, admitted: "My first thought was I'm not breastfeeding him!" He broke the previous world record of being born with eight teeth. Three days after he was born, the teeth were pulled to prevent possible feeding problems. *D.Mirror, 20 June 1990.*

SOMETHING ON HER MIND

A 17-year-old French girl, named only as Isabelle, was rushed to hospital when she started hallucinating. A brain scan showed a .22-calibre rifle bullet in her brain. Her mother recalled than when the girl was 15 months old, she came into the house with blood spurting from her head. She had called a doctor, who simply applied a bandage. *Leicester Mercury, 24 May 1995.*

THE TOOTH IS OUT THERE

Lan Riren, 91, from Bama county, Guangxi province, China, sprouted new teeth and found his white hair turned black after a mystery illness in July 1996 that left him unable to eat for 20 days. He was able to gather wood and farm like an able-bodied young man. (There are many cases of third dentition in the medical records). *Hong Kong Standard, 9 Oct 1996.*

EYE EYE... EYE

A hospital in Fujian, China, found that a man of 23 (or 25) named only as Deng, had three eyes, the first such case ever recorded in China. The third eye, on his left temple, had an eyebrow, eyelid, eyelashes, a tear gland and a pupil that moved in sync with his other eyes. However, Deng was blind in his left eye and the third eye. Shanghai's Xinmin Wanbo newspaper said that this was the third known case of a three-eyed person in the world. *Deutsche Presse-Agentur, 10 Feb 1997.*

HE'S GLOWING

A teenager in the central Vietnamese province of Ninh Thuan began to glow in the dark. Cha Ma Le Buot, 17, first noticed in February 1997 that his body was unusually warm and covered with spots giving off a bluish-white light which flickered and died. He experienced the symptoms nightly, although by day he appeared normal. He was said to be the third person to exhibit the symptoms – although other cases appear in Christian hagiography. *[AFP] 5 Mar 1997.*

HALE AND HEARTY

Doctors in Esztergom, Hungary, who treated a teenager stabbed in a fight, thought he would die because the knife had apparently penetrated his heart. However, the 18-year-old, identified only as VJ, had his heart on the right-hand side. "He was born under a lucky star," said a doctor as the youth recovered in hospital. *[AFP] 2 Oct 1997.*

PRESERVED PRELATE

Chrysostomos, abbot of the Panayia Galaktotrophousa monastery in the southern district of Larnaca in Cyprus, died in 1988 at the age of 79. His coffin was opened in 1991 in order to place his bones in an ossuary, but the monks found that he had not decomposed. They now revere him as a saint and are refusing to rebury him. Photographs printed by the *Politis* newspaper show Chrysostomos covered with white cloth sitting upright in a wooden box, with a withered hand poking out. *[R] 28 Sept 1999.*

BLOODY TEARS

Hind Medjhad, 23, a law student from Mascara in Algeria, who had been weeping blood for two months despite having apparently healthy eyes, was to be sent to see specialists in Saudi Arabia. Algerian doctors had found nothing to explain why musk-scented blood flowed regularly from her eyes. She had been hailed by some as having healing powers. *[AFP] 6 Mar 2000.*

WEEPING STONES

In February 2004, doctors in Saudi Arabia were investigating the case of Mara, an eight-year-old girl who had been weeping stones for the past month, according to the *Saudi Gazette*. The appearance of the stones had been recorded on video. Mara's father had counted eight stones the size of cereal grains. Analysis showed they consisted of calcium, magnesium, carbon and uric acid. *[ANP/DPA] 27 Feb 2004.*

GREEN SWEAT

A man from Guangzhou in China sought medical help after his sweat turned green. He first noticed the problem when his white T-shirts started turning green under his arms as soon as he put them on. Doctors speculated that it might be caused by a mystery parasite. A doctor at the Guangzhou Friendship Hospital said he had read of cases of red and blue sweat in ancient medical books but never green. *Ananova 7 June; News of the World, 13 June 2004.*

HORNY MAN

Olag Kravitzy, 42, was shunned in the streets because he has grown horns and looks like the devil. He had to have regular operations to trim off the 2.7in (7cm) horns after he started sprouting them seven years earlier in Ulan-Ude, Russia. "People shun me in the street," he said, "because they think I am Satan." A surgeon said: "The horns are similar to a bullock's and emerge from each temple on his head. It's a genetic throwback that has been triggered by pollution." *D.Mirror, 18 Jan 2000.*

Chapter 5

WHAT ARE THE ODDS?

These stories of brushes with death,
incredible coincidences, lucky streaks and
narrow escapes suggest that sometimes
you can buck the statistics – like the man
who survived not one but two earthquakes
that killed nearly 300,000 people.

COINCIDENCES

A CERTAIN SYMMETRY

A 39-year-old Singapore man whose life was saved by a tree after he fell from an apartment block in 1984 was killed when he was hit by a tree cut down by workers. *Straits Times (Singapore), via Edinburgh Eve. News, 19 Nov 1990.*

DOUBLE THE FUN

In 1991, the last time a Friday the 13th fell in September, Luisa Patterson, 33, of Holbrook, New York, gave birth to twins, a healthy boy and a girl. On 13th September 1996, she gave birth to a second pair of Friday 13th twins. She hadn't taken fertility drugs. *Newsday, 14 Sept 1996.*

POND GOODBYE

Freeman Whitney was a school director in Harrison, Maine, and a driving force behind the establishment of Mill Pond Park, a one-acre pond with a park in the centre of town. On 20 July 1997, the day Whitney died aged 74, Mill Pond mysteriously emptied itself. According to one resident, the pond drained because the dam below the pond developed a leak from repairs done three years earlier – but another confided: "They are saying that Freeman took the pond with him." *Portland (ME) Press-Herald, 26 July 1997.*

SUITS YOU

When Hilda Golding, 87, picked up her cards at a whist drive in the village hall at Bucklesham, near Ipswich in Suffolk, she found she had all 13 clubs. Hazel Ruffles, 64, had all the diamonds and her daughter, Alison Chilvers, 40, had all the hearts. The full suit of spades went to dummy. It was the first hand of the evening. The cards had been shuffled twice and cut. *D.Telegraph, D.Mirror, 27 Jan 1998.*

HOMING KEYS

A fireman called to break into a house surprised a couple by handing them the keys they had lost. John Pearson, 24, found them in the street on his way to the fire station in Birmingham. *D.Telegraph, 27 April 1999.*

LOTTO LUCK

A newspaper in Vancouver, Washington, published the numbers of a state lottery before it was drawn. *The Columbian* mistakenly printed the numbers for the Virginia draw instead of the one in Oregon, but hours later, the same numbers came out of the hat: 6-8-5-5. The paper's computers had crashed and there was a rush to recreate a page that had been lost. In the confusion, the Virginia numbers were inserted by mistake. Lottery organisers investigated and discovered the bizarre coincidence. *[AP] 4 July 2000.*

TRAVELLING BAND

As Dave Gould (36) and Katie Smith (27) did their holiday packing in Harrogate, North Yorkshire, in September 2000, she lost the gold and sapphire ring given to her by her grandmother. In four months, the couple travelled more than 10,000 miles (16,000km) in Egypt, USA and Costa Rica, trekking across desert and jungle and climbing mountains. Before flying home, Mr Gould cleaned his mud-caked Timberland boots, which he had worn almost continuously – and discovered the ring jammed in the boot's tread. *D.Mail, D.Record, 29 Jan 2001.*

ACTION REPLAY

Simon May, 20, from Hooe, Devon, broke his leg playing football for Plymstock United against Roborough in March 2003. The following October, he suffered the same injury to the same leg against the same team and the same opposition player – and was treated in the same hospital by the same nurse. *D.Express, 31 Oct 2003.*

CREATURES OF HABIT

Peter Keogh (64), his son Eric (40), and Eric's daughter Bethany (8), were all born on 29 February. They are quite possibly the only family in the world with three generations all born on Leap Day. *News of the World, 29 Feb 2004.*

" At the 16th hole, Brendan Quinn hit a shot that decapitated a flying robin "

HOLE UP AT HOME

Potholing couple Graham and Chrissy Price were digging foundations for a conservatory in their garden in Oakhill, Somerset, when the ground gave way and exposed a giant cave complex. Spelæologists believed it stretched for several hundred feet. The Prices didn't seem to mind losing their front garden. "An en-suite pot-hole is the ultimate thrill for any caver," said Graham, 53. *Times, Sun, 16 July 2005.*

TWO DOWN

Dublin photographer Ronan Quinlan and his golfing partner Brendan Quinn scored two birdies on a recent round – a robin and a seagull. At the 13th hole, Quinn hit a 5-iron second shot and hit a flying robin, decapitating it. On the 16th, a par five, Quinlan hit a second shot with a 3-wood. The ball struck a seagull, which fell dead on the fairway. *The Journalist, Dec 2005.*

BURNING ANNIVERSARY

A couple believed their historic thatched manor house might be cursed after it was devastated by fire eight years *to the day* after burning down in another blaze. Andrew and Nikki Reason, who bought 17th-century Bryar Cottage in Theale, Berkshire, for £750,000 in August 2004, were "confronted by devastation" when they came home from work on 31 January 2006. Both fires were believed to have been started by stray embers from log fires or stoves. *Metro, 2 Feb 2006.*

LIFE FOR A LIFE

Kevin Stephan, 17, of Buffalo, New York State, was working a dishwashing shift in a New York restaurant on 27 January when he was summoned to perform the Heimlich manoeuvre on Penny Brown, who was choking on her lunch. He didn't recognise her as the off-duty nurse who got his heart beating again after a bat hit him in the chest during a baseball game in July 1999. But Kevin's mother, who happened to be in the restaurant, knew who it was. "You saved my son's life seven years ago," said Lorraine Stephan, "and now he's saved yours." *Buffalo (NY) News, 5 Feb 2006.*

WHISKAS GALORE

A crashed lorry spilled 20 tons of cat food outside a cats' refuge. The charity in Bury St Edmunds, Suffolk, was allowed to keep the food. *News of the World, 12 Feb 2006.*

DOUBLE JEOPARDY

A South African man was carjacked in the same vehicle, on the same date and in the same place as he had been a year earlier. Two armed men jumped out from a car and threatened Ernest Ndlovu, 35, from Mpumalanga, before seizing his van and driving away. Police later recovered his van, as they had the first time round. *D.Telegraph, 29 Nov 2007.*

DANGEROUS LIAISONS

ROUND TWO

Martin Aurvaag, 55, a Norwegian fisherman, put an anonymous lonely hearts advertisement in his local paper and got a reply from his wife. A photograph of Lilly Jacobsen accompanied a letter starting with the words "Hello Unknown Friend". He began a new romance with his wife who unwittingly ended their 18-year separation by replying. The couple had had no contact for a decade. *[R] 30 Mar 1990.*

LYING ON THE BEACH

A Romanian couple were planning to divorce after they accidentally met on the beach at Mamaia on the Black Sea while chatting to each other on mobiles. Lucica Dragomirescu was telling her husband Victor that she was feeling ill and couldn't get out of bed; Victor was complaining about the amount of work he had to do at his parents' house. "I am all full of dust as I have just been to the mill in town," he said before he looked up and saw his wife in front of him. *Bournemouth Daily Echo, 24 July 2003.*

RECIPROCAL INFIDELITY

According to *Ma'ariv*, the Israeli daily, a Haifa woman published an anonymous lonely hearts ad in the local paper and received a reply from her own husband, after which the couple sought a divorce. The family court was trying to decide which partner was guilty of adultery. *Queensland Weekend Bulletin, 12-13 July 2003.*

CAUGHT IN THE NET

For months, Adnan and Jamila flirted on an Internet chatroom in Jordan. Finally, a romantic assignation was arranged at a bus station near Amman. It turned out that "Adnan" was really Bakr Melhem (or Melhelf) and "Jamila" was his wife, Sanaa (or Sana). He divorced her on the spot, she called him a liar, and then fainted. *Irish Independent, 12 Feb; Independent on Sunday, 13 Feb 2005.*

STRANGELY FAMILIAR

They cheated on each other – with each other. Sana Klaric, 27, and husband Adnan, 32, poured out their hearts online over their marriage troubles. Using the names 'Sweetie' and 'Prince of Joy', they told each other they had found their soul mate. They got a shock when they met in person near their home in Zenica, central Bosnia, and are divorcing after accusing each other of infidelity. Adnan said: "I still find it hard to believe that Sweetie, who wrote such wonderful things, is actually the same

woman I married and who has not said a nice word to me for years."
Metro, 18 Sept 2007.

NARROW ESCAPES

PRUDENT GESTURE

To appease Pele, the volcano goddess, a shopkeeper in Hawaii placed three leaves and a bottle of gin in the path of molten lava flowing from Mount Kilauea. After the lava had passed, all that was left of the town of 300 was a church and the prudent man's shop. *Nairobi Standard, 7 Jan 1991.*

THAT PUT THE WIND UP HIM

A gust of wind blew Aimé Grosjean, 72, off a balcony of a 17th floor apartment in Regensdorf, Switzerland. Luckily, another gust of wind blew him onto the balcony of the 16th floor apartment. He suffered no more than bruises and a cut to his arm. *Le Matin (Lausanne, Switzerland), 25 July 1995.*

PLANE LUCKY

Farmer Eldon Ferguson, 44, was flying with a friend from Quebec to Newfoundland in a hired Cessna when an explosion blew away the front of the aircraft. He fell 5,000ft (1,525m) and landed unhurt in a snow-drift. The two pilots, however, died. *D.Mail, 4 Nov 1997.*

CRASH SAVES LIFE

Prof. Ronald Mann, 77, from Waterlooville, Hampshire, had a heart attack while driving. As he slipped into unconsciousness, his Honda Civic smashed into a tree and he was thrown forward so hard into the steering wheel that it snapped in half. The impact had the effect of a defibrillator, jolting his heart back to life. Prof. Mann and his three passengers (who suffered cuts and bruises) were taken to hospital in Chichester, West Sussex. The professor, editor of a medical journal, hailed the "million-to-one" chance that saved his life. *D.Mail, 24 Mar 2006.*

DOUBLE PROTECTION

Bill Henry, 54, was saved from being shot when the bullet hit two New Testaments in his shirt pocket. He escaped with a bruise after two gunmen tried to kill him during a robbery at the Christian charity centre he runs in Orange Park, Florida. One rifle bullet passed through the first Bible and lodged in the second. *D.Mirror, 9 Nov 2006.*

CRAPPY LANDING

A Chinese woman was hanging out washing on her sixth floor balcony in Nanjing on 2 April 2007 when she lost her balance and fell to the ground. Luckily, her fall was broken by a pile of excrement 8in (20cm) deep, and she suffered only slight injuries. Workers happened to be emptying the building's septic tank, which had regularly blocked sewage pipes. The previous month, a six-year-old girl escaped with a broken leg when she fell six floors onto a pile of snow in the northeastern province of Heilongjiang. *[R] 4 April 2007.*

SOFT LANDING

A man who plummeted 25ft (9m) down a liftshaft survived after landing on an unconscious woman who had fallen down it a day earlier. Jens Wilhelms, 27, escaped from the void in his apartment block in Frankfurt, Germany, and called for help. The woman, 57, was critical in hospital. Rescue workers said that if she had not been found she would have died from internal bleeding. *Sun, 16 April 2008.*

O LUCKY MAN

Alatanbagan Taoqi, 60, was the only person left alive in his office block when it collapsed on 12 May 2008 in Beichuan during the Sichuan earthquake, which claimed 55,000 lives. In 1976 the former miner was close to the epicentre of the great Tanshan quake in northeast China that killed over 240,000 people. Back then, Taoqi was buried under rubble for 10 days. *D.Mirror, 24 May 2008.*

" Luckily, her fall was broken by a pile of excrement and she suffered only minor injuries "

REVENGE THWARTED

Miroslav Miljici, 46, tried to kill his mother-in-law, claiming she had broken up his marriage. He stood across the street from her house and fired an anti-tank missile into the ground floor living room. When he realised she was upstairs having a nap, he peppered her bedroom with a machine gun. A court in Doboj, Bosnia, heard that the 73-year-old had survived both attacks. Miljici was jailed for six years. *Sun, 31 Mar 2009.*

SAVED BY THE BELL

Barry Whitelaw was awakened about 6.45am on 3 August by a phone call to his house in Dinsdale, New Zealand. It was a wrong number, but Mr Whitelaw smelled smoke and found an electric heater on fire. He threw it on the lawn and doused it with water. Ringing back the mystery caller to thank him, he found it was an ex-firefighter from Tauranga called Wayne Kennedy, who had been trying to ring a radio station. *Waikato Times (NZ), 4 Aug 2009.*

LONG SHOTS

FATEFUL PHONECALL

Malca Cramer of Toronto placed a call to Edmonton and got a wrong number. The young woman on the line began crying and said: "Mom, it's me." It was her daughter who had run away three years earlier. They were subsequently reunited. *Toronto Star, 4 April 1986.*

THAT'S MY BIRD

Harry Walker, 69, of Belper in Derbyshire, tried to ring the police to see if there was any news of his pet falcon, Lenny, which had gone missing the day before (7 February 1995). He misdialled and spoke to a family in Wyver Lane, several streets away, who told him that the bird was perched on their fence. *Derby Eve. Telegraph, 10 Feb 1995.*

CELL MATES

A robber jailed for eight years in Argentina hired a detective to trace the father he had never met – and found it was the warden of his prison. *D.Mirror, 28 Sept 1995.*

WATCH IT

Nick Coomes, 18, lost his watch in a Jersey nightclub in August 1996. Two months later, on a train from London to his home in Salisbury, he asked a stranger the time and saw that she was wearing a watch just like his. The girl had also been in the nightclub on holiday and found the watch, which was engraved with his name. *Newcastle Journal, Times, 1 Nov 1996.*

NICE DEVELOPMENT

A man who lost his new camera in the mud at the Glastonbury Festival had it returned after a woman found it, developed the film and recognised him from one of the photographs on the dance floor of a club in

Nottingham. Kirsty Kelly-Lewin had picked up Andy Scothern's camera after losing hers in the same way. *Times, 27 Aug 1997.*

FITTING MEMENTO

Retired naval pilot John Crossley, 64, bought an Airfix model of a Sea Venom, the twin-tail jet he flew during a two-year stint on *HMS Albion* in the 1950s. He was astonished to discover it bore his service number – and his name. *D.Mirror, 10 May 2004.*

HOLIDAY SURPRISE

Tourist Alf Newman, 68, was stunned to find a taxi he took in Jamaica was the same Nissan Sunny he had scrapped 16 years earlier in Chichester, Sussex. *Sun, 12 Oct 2004.*

FATEFUL DINNER

On 11 August 2002, Kari Maracic was invited to dinner in San Francisco where she found herself sitting next to Ben Davis. She talked about the sadness of being unable to find her long-lost brother, which deepened as his birthday approached. Ben said he understood, as he had tried unsuccessfully to find his birth family. When he mentioned his birthday was 9 August 1968, it soon transpired they were siblings. Ben had been given up for adoption. *(Toronto) National Post, 21 June 2004.*

HIGHLAND LUCK

When his 1954 R-type Bentley broke down on a remote country road between Fort William and Loch Ailort in the Scottish Highlands, Bob Michie, 87, had it towed to a garage, where the problem was diagnosed as a broken rotary arm, which provided the spark to the distributor. The mechanics didn't have a spare and had no idea where to find one. They flagged down an AA van and, almost in jest, asked patrolman Mickey Miller if he had one. Amazingly, he did, having kept one in his van for 28 years "just in case". Mr Michie was back on the road within minutes. *D.Mail, 28 Oct 2005.*

ELECTIVE AFFINITIES

THE LORD GIVETH...

Steve Mallinson, 44, of Rickmansworth, Hertfordshire, won £371.70 on the football pools – and in the same post got a tax demand for £371.70. *D.Mirror, 2 Oct 1990.*

DOUBLE TROUBLE

A Citroen 2CV6 and a Triumph Acclaim collided in Winkfield, Berkshire, on 29 July 1992. The drivers were Mrs Kathleen Wolfenden, 52, a librarian from Ward Close, Wokingham, and Mrs Kathleen Wolfenden, 64, an ex-midwife from Poole in Dorset. They were unrelated. *D.Telegraph, 30 July; Bracknell News, 6 Aug 1992.*

FEARFUL SYMMETRY

Thomas Allen of Cliftonville, Kent, went to hospital for an operation on his left hand. In the waiting room he chatted to man with a similar ailment affecting his right hand. When a nurse asked for "Alan", they both answered. The other man's name: Alan Thomas. *Best, 10 Mar 1994.*

MICHELLE, MY BELLE

Mother-of-two Michelle Samways and mother-of-two Michelle Samways hadn't met when they moved into numbers 5 and 6 Longstone Close, Portland, Dorset, in October 1994. Hardly a day went by without a mix-up. The two women, aged 26 and 27, were of similar height, build and complexion; both were named after the 1965 Beatles song. *Western Daily Press, 2 June 1995.*

TRULY SINGULAR

Geoff Langlois hit a hole-in-one at the St Pierre Park golf course on Guernsey recently. On the same day, only three miles (4.8km) away at L'Ancresse golf course, another Geoff Langlois hit another hole-in-one. "I reckon trying to work out the odds on that would probably break the calculator," said a spokesman for the bookmakers Ladbrokes. *Guernsey Eve. Press, 31 May 1999.*

Chapter 6

HEAVENS ABOVE!

It's always worth keeping an eye on the
sky, as you never quite know what's going
to come flying out of it - rains of fish or
frogs, worms, crabs, giant chunks of ice,
airborne rabbits or even Superman!

LOOK OUT BELOW!

SWEDISH SURPRISE

A couple from Tomelilla in Sweden were driving down a road to Lake Snogeholm, south of Sjobo in Scania, when a large bream fell from the sky and smashed their windscreen. *Sydsvenskan (Sweden), 6 July 1991.*

RAINING FROGS AND TOADS

People in the Urziceni area of southern Romania woke up on 25 June 1997 after heavy overnight rain to find the ground ankle-deep in frogs. It was believed they had been sucked up by strong winds and carried long distances. At around 11pm on 5 July, motorists reported a shower of toads in Villa Angel Flores, near Culiacan on Mexico's Pacific coast. The newspaper *El Debate* maintained that a mini tornado had whirled them up from a nearby pond. *BBC Teletext, 26 July; [AP] 8 July 1997.*

CROP SPRAY

Gloria Daniels, 68, was working in her garden in Lusby, Maryland, with a young neighbour boy on 25 August 1997 when she was hit by a tomato. Then the boy was hit. More than 30 tomatoes landed in her yard, appearing to fall straight down from a clear sky. Friends, neighbours and the media investigated, but nobody could figure where the plummeting fruit were coming from. The reporter who filed the story was himself struck by a tomato. *Calvert County (MD) Recorder, 27 Aug 1997.*

HEAVENLY BALLS

Margaret Benvie, 28, escaped being hit by a small metal ball in Tullibody, Clackmannanshire. "A glint in the sky caught my eye and I was mesmerised," she said. "As I watched, this object fell. It just missed me and my husband and landed on our doorstep." She later discovered that her neighbour, Caroline Gear, 32, had found a similar object in her garden. "We don't know for sure what caused the incident," blustered a spokesman for the Ministry of Defence, obscurely. *D.Record, 25 Sept 1997.*

FALL OUT

Police in Western Australia were baffled after a small egg-shaped canister fell from the sky onto the small town of Muchea. Inspector Denis Perich said it wasn't space debris or radioactive. "The canister has disintegrated," he said, "but a farmer was able to take a sample of the liquid oozing from it. He described it as 'green bubbling fluid'." *[AFP] 9 Nov 1997.*

ANCHOVY RAIN

When Kate Duckworth returned home from work on 27 October 1999, she discovered about 50 small anchovies scattered around her yard and on her roof in Sausalito, California. A physicist colleague at the Exploratorium, a hands-on science museum in San Francisco where she worked, put forward – without any evidence – the theory that a water-spout was responsible. *Arkansas Democrat-Gazette, 12 Nov 1999.*

SINGULAR MISSILE

Workers at Waterloo station, investigating damage to the glass roof of the Eurostar terminal, found the remains of a reindeer's leg. "Damage to the panels can be caused by anything from birds carrying things to pieces falling off aeroplanes," said a spokesman. "I can confirm that a reindeer's hoof was found. How it got there, I could not begin to specu-late." *Times, 3 Mar 2000.*

COSMIC CRAPOLA

Late on the night of 29 September 2000, strange reddish-brown sludge rained down on houses in Middleton, Idaho (pop: 1,851). Tests showed that it wasn't waste from an aircraft and government officials were unable to say where it came from. *Canadian Business, 30 Oct 2000.*

BOUNCING CHEQUE

Gary Howard was driving a tractor on his dairy farm in Long Lane, Missouri, on a calm clear day last December when a cheque fell from the sky. He traced the owner to Stark City, Missouri, about 100 miles

" How do you explain to the FAA that we had a rabbit strike at 1,800 feet? "

(160km) away. The day before, a furious storm had swept through the town, tearing up buildings and carrying off debris. Curiously, the cheque was completely dry. *Times, 6 Jan 2003.*

FISH FALL

A number of small fish (species unspecified) fell on the streets of Knighton, Powys, mid-Wales, at about 2.30pm on 18 August 2004 during a brief thunderstorm. Some were still alive. Meteorologists presumed they had been sucked up from the River Teme by a whirlwind – although (as usual) no whirlwind had been observed. *Shropshire Star, 19 Aug; D.Express, 21 Aug 2004.*

CRAB FALL

Kate Walker, 33, was pelted with crabs during a freak storm in Dartford, Kent, in late October. At first she thought the crustaceans were just heavy raindrops as she pottered in her garden; but she soon saw 20 crabs crawling on the grass. The customary "tornado" explanation was trotted out. *Metro, 22 Oct 2004.*

ICE STOPPED PLAY

Sunday, 22 May 2005 was a warm, sunny day, but at 6.30pm a village cricket match at Davington near Faversham, Kent, was interrupted when a huge chunk of ice fell onto the pitch and exploded, spreading slush across the ground about 10ft (3m) square. It missed the umpire by 10ft. The sky was cloud-free and no aircraft was in view. Similar ice missiles of meteoric origin – called megacryometeors – caused extensive damage in Spain and Italy in 2000. Analysis ruled out ice from aircraft, hailstones or even mini-comets. *Times, 6 June 2005.*

FROG RAIN

Traffic came to a halt and locals fled inside after thousands of frogs fell from the sky onto the village of Odzaci in Serbia, 75 miles (120km) northwest of Belgrade, on 5 June 2005. The frogs, different from those usually seen in the area, survived the fall and hopped around in search of water. "This huge 'cloud' seemed to come out of nowhere and its shape and colour looked very strange," said Caja Jovanovic. "Suddenly frogs started to fall from the sky. I thought maybe a plane carrying frogs had exploded in midair." A local climatology expert repeated the by-now traditional 'whirlwind' explanation. *South African Press Association, Ananova, 7 June 2005.*

FLYING RABBIT

The Smithsonian Institution's Feather Identification Laboratory regularly receives tissue swabs from bird-plane collisions. The bloody goo is nicknamed "snarge". It's not just birds. "We've had frogs, turtles, snakes," said Carla Dove, the lab's director. "We had a cat once that was struck at some high altitude. The other day we sent a sample to the DNA lab and it came back as rabbit. How do you explain to the FAA that we had a rabbit strike at 1,800ft [550m]?" Hawks and herons occasionally drop their quarries into incoming planes. *Wired News, 23 Sept 2005.*

THE EAST IS RED

Thousands of worried people in the northern regions of Russia's Far Eastern Maritime territory phoned emergency services on 13 March after red snow fell. Meteorologists said it was caused by red sand picked up in neighbouring Mongolia by a powerful cyclone. A month earlier, yellow snow with a strong odour and oily texture fell on Russia's Far East island of Sakhalin. This was either caused by industrial pollution or maybe by volcanic activity. *MosNews, 13 Mar 2006.*

MANNA FROM HEAVEN

There's been a fish fall in the south-western Indian state of Kerala in... (wait for it) the village of Manna. Small, pencil-thin live fish falling from the sky. "Initially no one noticed it, but soon we saw slushy objects on the ground and noticed movement," Abubaker, a shopkeeper, told the *Hindustan Times*. "I alone collected 30 ice-cold fish." *(London) Eve. Standard, 24 July; Metro, 25 July 2006.*

ICE PUNCHED THROUGH

A mysterious hole was found in the ice of a pond in Latvia on 4 February 2007. Despite sub-zero temperatures, the small hole remained unfrozen for two days. There had been reports of a small bright object falling from the sky and beams of light emerging from the hole. A meteorite might explain the bright object, but not the light beams or the hole's longevity. *Times, 24 Feb 2007.*

ICE METEORITES

A giant ice ball that fell out of a clear sky in a Johannesburg suburb on 7 July 2006 hadn't fallen from an aircraft but was a megacryometeor. The impact created a small crater in a parking lot, which was left covered with ice fragments. Another one, weighing 44lb (20kg), fell on a building in Madrid in Spain on 15 March 2007. *Spokane (WA) Spokesman-Review, 16 July 2006; Irish Star, 16 Mar 2007.*

RAINING WORMS

Police employee Eleanor Beal was crossing a street in Jennings, Louisiana, on her way to work when large clumps of tangled worms fell from the sky. "When I saw that they were crawling, I said, 'It's worms! Get out of the way!'", she said. Some believe that a waterspout spotted near Lacassine Bayou less than five miles away at that same time could have something to do with it. *WAFB (Baton Rouge, LA), 11 July; Times, 14 July 2007.*

PUNCHING THE ICE

Residents of Spruce Grove in Alberta, Canada, woke on 20 January

2008 to an octopus-shaped hole in a frozen golf-course pond. It was about 5ft (1.5m) in diameter, with at least 20 splash marks up to 20ft (6m) long. Astronomer Martin Beech didn't rule out a meteorite, but the marks perplexed him.

To punch through ice 20in (50cm) thick, the meteorite would have to have been huge – a burning ball with a sonic boom – but no one saw or heard a thing. *MX News (Brisbane), 21 Jan 2008.*

BAD DAY FOR GOOSE

One morning, postman Adrian Mannion and his wife Fiona, of Elstree, Derbyshire, heard "two almighty thuds" and rushed out to see a 9lb (4kg) meteorite next to their Mini and a mangled Canada Goose on the car's roof. It appeared the goose had been hit by the meteorite and smashed into the roof, causing £2,500 damage. A fox then dragged away the goose before they could rescue it. The University of Derby was studying the meteorite. *Sun, 5 Feb 2008.*

AIM FOR LAJIC

Radivoje Lajic has had the roof of his house in Gornja Lamovite, northern Bosnia, reinforced with steel girders after it was struck five times by meteorites since November 2007, always during heavy rain. "I am obviously being targeted by extraterrestrials," he said. "I don't know what I have done to annoy them."

Experts at Belgrade University confirmed the meteoric origin of the rocks and were investigating local magnetic fields. *D.Mail, 10 April 2008.*

INJURED BY ICE

A 6lb (2.7kg) chunk of ice fell from the sky and through the roof of a house in York, Pennsylvania, on 8 October. It then punched a hole through a bedroom ceiling. One piece broke off and hit Mary Ann Foster, 66, on the forehead as she slept, causing an impressive swelling. She said the ice had a slightly fishy smell and looked like quartz. It was thought to have come from a plane or a rocket. *[AP] York (PA) Dispatch, 9 Oct 2008.*

LIGHTNING

THAT FIGURES

Tribesman Simphiwe Khosa was cleared by a court in Johannesburg of possessing 80lb (36kg) of cannabis after he told the judge it was for burning during thunderstorms – to ward off lightning. *The People, 27 June 1993.*

HIT THE HOLLANDS

A Texas teacher was the third member of her family to be hit by lightning. Debbie Holland's mother-in-law was in a coma for weeks after being struck by lightning as a child. Then Holland's husband was hit and tossed 60ft (18m) in the air. Finally, Holland herself was hit, throwing her 20ft (6m). *[AP] 21 Mar 1999.*

APT ZAP

Towering Inferno, the horse that played Phar Lap in the 1983 film about Australia's greatest racehorse, was killed by lightning in a hailstorm in Sidney on 14 April 1999. Phar Lap means lightning in the Sri Lankan language Sinhalese. The gelding was discovered two days later by his owner Heath Harris. *Melbourne Herald Sun, 17 April 1999.*

FOURTH TIME LUCKY

Mark Stenton survived being struck by lightning for the fourth time on 3 August 2002. He was working on his truck at home in Chatham County, North Carolina, when the strike knocked him out. The soles of his shoes burned off and his watch melted. "I either draw it or I've got the worst luck anybody can possible have – I haven't decided which," he said. *Local 6 News, Ananova, 7 Aug 2002.*

ACT OF GOD

A guest evangelist, preaching repentance at the First Baptist Church in Forest, Hardin County, Ohio, on 2 July 2005, was struck by lightning moments after asking God for a sign. The thunderbolt hit the church

" When he was struck by lightning, smoke was seen coming out of the actor's ears "

steeple, blew out the sound system and enveloped the preacher, who was unhurt. The church, however, was set on fire, causing damage estimated at $20,000. *[AP] 4 July 2003.*

DIVINE WARNING

Jim Caviezel, the actor playing Jesus in Mel Gibson's film *The Passion of the Christ*, which has drawn complaints from religious leaders, escaped injury after being struck by lightning during filming. Smoke was seen coming out of his ears. The bolt also hit the umbrella of assistant director Jan Michelini, who had already suffered light burns on the tips of his fingers when struck by an early bolt during filming on a hilltop months earlier. *[AP] BBC News, 23 Oct; NY Post, 24 Oct 2003.*

MARKED MAN

A Cuban farm worker was struck by lightning for the fifth time in 22 years. Jorge Marquez, who works in San Manuel, was first struck in June 1982. His hair was burnt and all his dental fillings fell out. The last time he was struck he managed to minimise the damage by grabbing a piece of rubber to insulate him as soon as it started to rain. He said he was cursed and that lightning followed him. US park ranger Roy Sullivan (1912-83) holds the record – he was struck seven times before committing suicide. *Ananova, 27 Sept 2004.*

LIGHTNING CONDUCTOR

Jorge Marquez, a Cuban farmer, has been struck by lightning five times in the last 22 years. When he is hit, he feels "like something very cold enters my body or as if I'm a hot iron being immersed in cold water". *New York Post, 27 Feb 2005.*

FUQING LIGHTNING

Mr Huang went to see Mr Xu in Fuqing city, China, to demand the return of 500 yuan (£40) borrowed three years earlier. "I told him that if he dared to swear to God that he didn't owe me the money, then I would waive his debt," said Huang. Xu made the oath in front of a crowd of neighbours and one minute later was struck by lightning. He was expected to recover. *North-West Eve. Mail, 1 Sept 2008.*

FLYING MEN

AERIAL LAW MAN

Hundreds of people in the small Serbian town of Ljubovija reported seeing a cloaked figure "flying as if he had an invisible engine on his back" and changing direction apparently at will, the local newspaper *Blic* reported. They speculated that he was a Superman-style crime fighter searching for the fugitive leader Radovan Karadzic, wanted for war crimes. *(London) Eve. Standard, 25 Aug 2005.*

IT'S SUPERMAN!

Twenty villagers from Gemeni in Romania are convinced they have seen Superman in his famous blue suit. "Reliable citizens saw him flying over their houses," said police officer Ion Anuta. Constantin Toader, 41, said: "He looked like Superman and was flying slowly at about 100 yards [91m] from the ground in a standing position." *Sunday Mail, 23 Sept 2007.*

Chapter 7

CRIMINAL CAPERS

Crime doesn't pay – at least not for
our collection of cretinous crooks,
bungling burglars and mad miscreants.
And what about the mugger who
gave his victims money, or the
drug smuggler who reported his
missing stash to the police?

CRIMINAL CRACKPOTS

IRISH JOKER

The accent gave Irishman Brendan Malony away in Birmingham when he tried to cash a Giro cheque made out to Abdul Khaliq. A birth certificate with Maloney crossed out and Khaliq written in didn't help. He was fined £100. *D.Mail, 21 June 1984.*

HE STUCK AROUND

Edilber Guimaraes, 19, was arrested in Belo Horizonte, Brazil, in November 1993 for attempted theft at a glue factory. He had stopped to sniff some of the glue he was stealing, keeled over and spilt two cans, sticking himself to the floor. He was found 36 hours later and had to be cut loose by firemen. *[R] 5 Nov 1993.*

DEAF TO REASON

Klaus Schmidt, 41, burst into a Berlin bank with a pistol and screamed: "Hand over the money!" Staff asked him if he wanted a bag, to which he replied: "Damn right, it's a real gun!". Sensing Schmidt was deaf, the manager set off the alarm. "It was ridiculously loud, but he didn't seem to notice." After five minutes, punctuated by Schmidt occasionally shouting: "I am a trained killer!" police arrived and arrested him. *Wolverhampton Express & Star, 23 Aug 1995.*

BURGER ME

A man walked into a Burger King in Ypsilanti, Michigan, at 7.50am, flashed a gun and demanded cash. The clerk said he couldn't open the cash register without a food order. When the man ordered onion rings, the clerk said they weren't available for breakfast. Frustrated, the man walked away. *Ann Arbor News,* via *Guardian, 6 Nov 1996.*

QUITE CUCKOO

Barry Parks, 35, walked out of Somewhere Antiques, Winchester, carrying a cuckoo clock. When picked up by the police shortly afterwards, he said he had taken the clock to release the cuckoo. Appearing before

Basingstoke magistrates, his defence was that he had taken three very strong LSD tablets before the incident. *Hampshire Chronicle, 16 May 1997.*

WHISTLER'S BOTHER

A gunman who had held up 21 people and forced them to whistle *Hail, Hail, the Gang's All Here* was being hunted in Alaska. He had never hurt anyone or stolen any property. *(Scottish) Sunday Mail, 8 Feb 1998.*

THEY MUST NEED GLASSES

Burglars trying to drill their way into an electrical goods store in Vara, Sweden, broke through the wall but found they were in an opticians instead. So they tried again and broke through to the opticians again. After four attempts they burst into the electrical shop, but an alarm went off and they fled empty-handed. *Sunday Times, 13 July 2003.*

POINTLESS HIJACK

In 1999, 15 minutes before a British Airways plane was due to land, Auburn Mason, 62, grabbed a stewardess, threatened her with scissors and said he would blow up the plane unless he was flown to Gatwick. This year, he was sentenced to four years in jail. It was all rather unnecessary, as the plane was heading for Gatwick anyway. *Xit (Aland, Finland), May 2003.*

BLUNDERING PIRATE

Trading standard officials were surprised when a young man cycled up to their headquarters on Beehive Lane, Chelmsford, Essex, and asked if they were interested in buying pirate DVDs. He had clearly failed to spot a large Trading Standards sign at the entrance. He fled when he realised his error, but left behind a bag with 150 DVDs and £210 in cash. He was tracked by CCTV. *Metro, 7 July 2004.*

DOPEY PASSENGER

When he returned from getting a beer in the main bus station in Campinas, a Brazilian man found that his two bags stuffed with nearly 125kg (276lb) of cannabis were missing, so he went to the police

> ❝ **When the back of the TV was unscrewed, the burglar was found curled up inside** ❞

station nearby to seek assistance. He was arrested straight away as the police had just collected the strongly smelling, unattended bags from the platform. *Ananova, 4 Feb 2004.*

HIDING IN TV

Alfred Blane, 45, a 6ft (1.8m) tall suspected burglar, went on the run for four months – but was captured on 14 January 2005 in a mobile home in Bainbridge, Georgia, after a tip-off. Searches in a freezer and a washing machine drew a blank, but a police dog kept going back to the TV. When the back was unscrewed, Blane was found curled up inside. *Augusta (GA) Chronicle, 16 Jan 2005.*

DIMWIT DRUG SMUGGLER

Leroy Carr stashed 68lb (31kg) of cocaine in two backpacks near a Boy Scout camp at the US-Canadian border on 3 August 2007. When he returned to pick up the backpacks, he found they had gone, so he called the police to see if they could help. He was told that he faced 10 years in jail. *Metro, 21 Sept 2007.*

BENEVOLENT BANDITS

ASHES RIDDLE

Someone broke into a house in Renfrew, Scotland, but didn't steal anything. He or she left behind a casket containing the ashes of a woman called Georgina D Collingwood. Police were baffled. *Edinburgh Eve. News, 7 Aug 1992.*

MUGGER MUDDLED

After he had been robbed of $20 in Winnipeg, Canada, Roger Morse asked for his wallet back. The mugger agreed, handed over his own wallet by mistake, ran off – and Mr Morse was $250 better off. *D.Record, 13 Mar 1993.*

MUST BE MAD

A 41-year-old man stood outside the Hong Kong stock exchange hand-ing out banknotes to passers-by, shouting at people to line up. He had about £8,000 in his pockets when he was hauled away for psychiatric examination. *[AP] 18 June 1993.*

ANTI-MUGGER

Police in Jamaica were baffled by a mugger who assaulted people and then stuffed $30 into their pockets before running away. *(Scottish) Sunday Mail, 8 June 1997.*

DRIVEN TO DISTRACTION

A car stolen in Lewes, Sussex, was eventually returned to its owner with a full tank of petrol, a new battery, the ignition and stereo speak-ers repaired, and a selection of new cassettes. *Guardian, 10 June 1998.*

HOUSEWORK BY STEALTH

Ataya Rsaya, 31, was arrested in Los Angeles for burglary. He had reportedly broken into homes and, before leaving with valuables, had often cleaned clothes, fixed dinners, sat by a fireplace with a glass of wine and re-arranged furniture.

Later that same year, German police were searching for a gang who raided houses and spent hours mopping, polishing and dust-ing. Nothing was ever taken except some food from the fridge. *[AFP] 18 Jan; Sunday Mail, 13 June 1999.*

UPBEAT OUTLAWS

Six men took over the Mashreq Bank in Nairobi, Kenya, for three hours, robbing customers as they arrived. They entertained their victims by singing hymns as they waited for their next victims to arrive. Before leaving, they invited their victims to a party at a city hotel to celebrate their newfound wealth. *Daily Nation (Nairobi), c.19 Aug 1999.*

DINING OUTLAW

Police in the Strausberg area of Germany were hunting a thief who broke into bungalows where he made himself dinner, washed up and left clean plates and an empty fridge. They believed he may have struck 200 times. *Boston (MA) Metro, 15 Nov 2001.*

ROBIN HOODLUM

An intruder who broke into a house in Charmouth, Dorset, stole nothing, but left behind a television and a bottle of alcopop. *Western Daily Press, 4 Jan 2002.*

JUST BORROWED

Thieves who stole a tree from a garden in Telford, Shropshire, returned a few days later and replanted it. *Shropshire Star, 29 Mar 2002.*

GOT CLEAN AWAY

Police in Mandeville, Louisiana, were hunting for a burglar who broke into houses, showered and left money behind. In one incident, he took in a basket of strawberries someone had left on the doorstep, used the shower and changed his clothes, leaving $50 and his dirty outfit behind. *Western Daily Press, 18 April; Irish Independent, 19 April 2003.*

FUEL PHANTOM

After author Mark Hatwood, 47, filled up his VW Polo with petrol at a Sainsbury's store in Truro, Cornwall, a masked woman approached him and said she was the Fuel Phantom. "I'd like to pay for your petrol," she said, before taking care of the £37.02 bill. "I felt like I'd been visited by an angel," said Mr Hatwood. *Metro, 12 Sept 2008.*

GNOME AFFAIRS

GO GNOME

Municipal workers found 119 garden gnomes in a wood near Aix and took them to Aix police station. They were believed stolen from Limoges by France's shadowy Gnome Liberation Front, which campaigns to free gnomes from "slavery and oppression". *D.Telegraph, 28 June 1997.*

GNOME SICK

Eleven garden gnomes were found hanging from a bridge in the French village of Briey. Police found a suicide note in which the gnomes said they wanted to "quit this world" and join a "sect of the temple of submissive dwarves". An offshoot of the defunct Gnome Liberation Front was suspected. *Sunday Times, 30 Aug; Guardian, 3 Sept 1998.*

WANDERING GNOMES

On 9 August 2002, a French mushroom picker discovered 101 gnomes arranged in a circle, some on tree stumps, in a pine forest near Podensec, south of Bordeaux. A further 112 gnomes were found beside a pond in Tamniès in the Dordogne on 20 August, and 30 in a school courtyard in Argentan, in the department of Orne, on 3 September. Meanwhile in Australia, 18 turned up on the steps of the Melbourne State Library on 23 August. *Ananova, 10 Aug; Melbourne Herald Sun, 25 Aug; Guardian, 5 Sept 2002.*

ALL DRESSED UP

FANCY THAT!

A suburban Mexico City bank was held up by midgets in fancy dress. Two gorillas, Spiderman and an octopus burst in, armed with knives and rifles, and told customers to lie on the floor before making off with $6,000 in a car driven by the Pope. They were members of a travelling circus taking advantage of recent civil unrest. *The Big Issue, 8-14 Feb 1994.*

OVERDRESSED

A man who knocked out gorillas with tranquilliser darts and then dressed them in clown outfits was being hunted in Kampala, Uganda. Later came news that John Ofosu was pulled over for speeding in his Ford Escort in Ghana. "I thought the family in the car were all very ugly," policeman Mustapha Garbah told a court in Accra. "Then I saw that the 14 passengers were all pregnant goats in T-shirts." Ofosu admitted stealing the animals in the Ashanti region. *Coventry Eve. Telegraph, 24 Feb; D.Star, Sun, 4 July; Big Issue, 5 July 1994.*

A FINE MOUSSAKA

French police were hunting a bank robber who dressed up as a giant aubergine. In the first heist in Marseilles, the bank manger asked: "Are you serious?" "No, I'm an aubergine," came the angry reply as the vegetable let off a shot. Staff handed over the cash. As he left, the robber deposited a real aubergine on the counter. There had been three further raids by the aubergine. *(London) Eve. Standard, 19 April 1996.*

FANCY LIVESTOCK

While pursuing a complaint from a farmer in Chaguanas, central Trinidad, that someone had stolen his livestock, police chased a rental car with its headlights off. The driver escaped, and police found a goat wearing a shirt, pants and a hat and a sheep wearing a dress in the back seat. There were two more goats – in shirts and pants – in the trunk. *Orange County (CA) Register, 16 May 1999.*

MAD MISDEMEANOURS

SWEDE REPLACED

A man from Kalmar, Sweden, returned home from work one day in November 1999 to find his door key didn't work and his name plate had been replaced by another name. Ringing the bell, he found an

" Around 2,000 baboon noses were found in plastic bags in an abandoned suitcase "

unknown woman and two children "living" in his flat. She claimed it was hers and refused him entry. She stuck by her story when the police were called. Finally, the landlord was called and the woman was evicted. The man said there were moments when he doubted that he really did live there. *Expressen (Sweden), 7 Nov 1999.*

HOPEFUL FANG

Chinese police detained a group of peasants after they claimed that a creature they were leading through the streets of Ziangcheng in Henan province in chains was a yeti. The parade ended abruptly when officers detained the "yeti" and his handlers as they asked passers-by for cash. It turned out to be a diminutive villager named Fang Xiwang, or Hopeful Fang, dressed in black fur. *D.Telegraph, 16 Feb 2000.*

SNIFFED OUT

Around 2,000 baboon noses were found in plastic bags in an abandoned suitcase at Amsterdam's Schiphol airport after they started to stink. Baboons are protected under international law. The noses, probably intended for consumption or for use in traditional medicines, were en route from Lagos to the United States. They were destroyed. *[AP] 3 Sept 2003.*

LEGLESS ESCAPE

Francois Johannes Pieterse, serving a 10-year sentence in Durban, South Africa, for fraud and impersonating a doctor, was taken to hospital in July, but escaped "unnoticed" even though he had no legs. "Two months later he is still 'on the run' and the authorities appear to be stumped," the *Saturday Star* reported. *Adelaide Sunday Mail, 14 Sept 2003.*

BARGAIN GRANDSON

Finding he had no money after putting petrol in his motorbike at a roadside stall, a Cambodian man left his nine-year-old nephew Dy as surety, promising to return with the 90p he owed. Nearly two years later, the old woman who sold the petrol was still waiting. She was keeping the boy and raising him as her grandson. *(London) Eve. Standard, 1 Dec; Metro, Queensland Times, 3 Dec 2003.*

BUG BUST

Hong Kong police smashed the second illegal insect-fighting gambling ring in a month after arresting 43 people for betting on battles between pet crickets. The men, aged between 48 and 73, were arrested in a swoop on the same building in Kowloon where 115 were arrested for the same offence in mid-August. *Gold Coast Bulletin, 22 Sept 2004.*

SNAIL SMUGGLER

A Nigerian woman, Surat Oluyemisi Anibaba, 42, arriving from Lagos, was stopped and searched at Heathrow airport on 3 March 2005 and was found to be carrying well over her own weight in edible snails. The haul, thought to be specimens of the giant African snail *Achatina achatina*, weighed 229lb (104kg). Anibaba was fined £400 with £65 costs. *D.Mail, 8 Mar; Guardian, 8+10 Mar 2005.*

BREAST ATTACK

A woman squirted her breast milk at a store detective when he tried to stop her pinching goods in Leicester. She exposed her breasts and fired away after being confronted in a Co-op store. The attack was thought to

" She exposed her breasts and fired away after being confronted in a Co-op store "

be the latest in a trend among shoplifters to get their DNA on security officers so that they can accuse them of sexual assault if caught. *Metro, 21 Sept 2007.*

BUNGLED BANK JOB

A Chinese burglar was jailed for a year after breaking into a bank and stealing forged notes. Zhan Chiu took £1,000 of cash that had been confiscated by the bank in the eastern province of Jiangxi and was ear-marked for shredding. He was caught when he tried to spend the duds. *Metro, 15 June 2009.*

CREATIVE CRIMES

SOUND OF SILENCE

Police in Germany were baffled by a wave of accordion-stabbings. A person or persons unknown broke into 11 Bonn music stores and plunged butcher's knives into the instruments. *(Scottish) Sunday Mail, 26 June 1994.*

MANGE TOUT

Turkish police were hunting a woman who raided flower shops in Ankara and fled after eating the heads off roses. Not long after, a man was undergoing psychiatric tests after breaking into a model's home in Bangkok and eating nine silk dresses. *Sunday Mail, 17 Sept, 8 Oct 1995.*

COP CLONES

Police in São Paulo, Brazil, discovered a fake police station only 100 metres (330ft) from a real one. It had fake policemen and detectives who charged high fees from everyone who needed their services. The real police were tipped off when two men who were blackmailed in the fake station made a complaint. Everybody in the fake station was arrested. *Ananova, 8 Feb 2003.*

FAUX ADMIN

A fake government office in northern India collected taxes, provided civic services and even handed out birth and death certificates. The *Times of India* said an office was set up outside Jhansi town in Uttar Pradesh state and 20 people employed in jobs such as street-sweeping. The scam came to light after some employees complained about salary problems to superiors in the actual government department. *(Brisbane) Courier-Mail, 11 Dec 2007.*

BELL HOPS IT

Thieves made off with a 658lb (298kg) copper bell from the top of a church tower in Kehidakustany, Hungary. "We cannot fathom it out," said a police spokesman. "The bell was almost 70ft [21m] up the tower and it would have taken a crane and dozens of men to get that down – but on one saw or heard anything." *North West Eve. Mail, 24 June 2008.*

Chapter 8

CRAZY CULTURE

From the Norwegian artist who
planned a version of Big Brother
using birds instead of people to the
man who lived on a diet of lizards
and petrol, some of these stories
are anything but high culture
or haute cuisine...

ARTSHOLES

THAT'LL LEARN THEM

Anti-sexists stole 300 Barbie and Duke dolls from New York stores, switched their voice-boxes and replaced them on the shelves. This left the Barbie dolls saying "Eat lead, Cobra!" and "Vengeance is mine!" while the macho Duke said "Let's plan a dream wedding" and "Let's go shopping". *D.Telegraph, 1 Jan 1994.*

MONEY FOR NOTHING

Art dealer John Austin advertised in a Sydney, Australia, newspaper that he would supply "absolutely nothing" for one dollar; and 489 people replied enclosing the cash. *News of the World, 12 May 1996.*

EXPENSIVE BLOB

A tiny blob of yellow household gloss paint by Damien Hirst, a fragment on one of his spot paintings (more than likely painted by a lowly assistant), was sold for $6,000 to Miuccia Prada of the Milan-based fashion empire. *D.Telegraph, 24 June 1997.*

BUILDING A REPUTATION

More than 10,000 people a month were visiting the World Brick Museum in Maizuru, Japan, to see 16 bricks from Scotland Yard, Covent Garden, the Albert Hall and St Pancras Station. Bricks and stones from the Anglican cathedral and dockyard at Portsmouth, a city twinned with Maizuru, were to be added to the exhibition. It was hoped that these would attract Japanese tourists to Portsmouth. *D.Telegraph, 5 May 1998.*

WORTH ITS WEIGHT IN GOLD

A small tin of excrement, one of eight works by Piero Manzoni, an Italian conceptual artist who died in 1963, was auctioned for £17,250 at Sotheby's in London on 2 July 1998. Manzoni produced a series of 90 tins of *merda d'artista*, labelled in English, French, German and Italian. Each tin of shit was signed, numbered and priced according to the daily market rate for gold. *[PA] 3 July 1998.*

POSTMODERN STUNT

Brendan San, a 21-year-old student, was shortlisted for an international prize in Norwich. His work consisted of two cheques each for £1,000 made out to the two judges. *Sunday Telegraph, 16 April 2000.*

FAKE DADA

London's Tate Modern Gallery is exhibiting the famous urinal, exhibited by Marcel Duchamp in 1917, entitled "Fountain" and signed "R. Mutt" ... except that the original was lost and a collector commissioned, not another common-or-jardin pissoir, but a faithful reconstruction, which the Tate bought in 1999. Duchamp would surely have laughed. *New Scientist, 27 Jan 2001.*

FEATHER BRAINED

"One could call it art, but for me it is a social realistic experiment with birds," said Magne Klann, a Norwegian artist who was staging an online version of Big Brother with birds instead of people. *Independent, – April 2003.*

PERILS OF ART COLLECTING

Actress Gina Gershon recently spent £50,000 on two bullet-riddled phone directories by the conceptual artist Tom Sachs. No sooner had she put them on display than her cleaner threw them out and replaced them with two brand new phone books. *The Week, 13 Mar 2004.*

DOLL ISLAND

The Mexican government has provided funds to build a museum on a small island in Teshuilo Lake, Mexico City, where the late Julian Santana, the sole inhabitant, tied thousands of dolls to trees. For 50 years, he scoured rubbish dumps for dolls and exchanged his homegrown vegetables for dolls from local people.

"On full moon nights you see small animals coming out of the dolls' mouths," said journalist Sebastian Flores. "It is a bit terrifying." *Ananova, 7 April 2004.*

" Six footballs were chained to lampposts alongside the message 'Can you kick it?' "

HARDBALL

During the World Cup, six footballs were chained to lampposts and trees around Berlin alongside the spray-painted message: "Can you kick it?" When they tried, two young men suffered broken toes and a third severe bruising – the balls were filled with concrete. Soon afterwards, two members of an Austrian art group called Mediengruppe LM/N were arrested. Their performance art piece – a "symbolisation of the mass phenomenon poured in concrete" – was not meant to cause injury, they said. *Metro, 5 July; The Australian, 10 July 2006.*

TEXAN LUNACY

After Texas schoolteacher Sydney McGee took her class of 10-year-olds to the Dallas Museum of Art, a parent complained that her child had seen "nude art" (statues without clothes). Ms McGee was suspended, told her contract would not be renewed, barred from transferring to another school and her post was advertised. More than 500,000 children had visited the museum in the last decade without complaint. *Independent on Sunday, 15 Oct 2006.*

STOP RIGHT THERE!

Demonstrators marched through the streets of Nantes in France on New Year's Eve carrying banners reading "No to 2007" and "Now is better".

They called on the UN to stop the "mad race" of time and declare the indefinite suspension of the future. Fonacon, the group that organised the protest, said that the ending of a year is another step towards the grave and therefore a tragedy, not a cause for joy. *Independent, 9 Dec 2006; Scotsman, 2 Jan 2007.*

BIZARRE BOOKS

ESSENTIAL REFERENCE

1991 saw the publication in Canada of *What Bird Did That?* "the world's first full-colour guide to identifying bird droppings". Perhaps the psychiatric profession could put it to use. Those Rorschach inkblots have become such a cliché. *Times, 27 Aug 1991.*

TITLE FIGHT

The 1995 winner of *The Bookseller*'s Diagram Prize for the Oddest Title of the Year went to *Re-using Old Graves* by D Davis and A Shaw. Runners-up included: *The Baby Jesus Touch and Feel Book*; *Simply Bursting: A Guide to Bladder Control*; *Searching for Railway Pole Insulators*; and *The History of the Concrete Roofing Tile*. A memorable previous winner was *How to Avoid Huge Ships. Guardian, Western Morning News, 3 Nov 1995.*

FURTHER WINNERS

Bombproof Your Horse by Rick Pelicano and Lauren Tjaden won the 2004 Diagram Prize. Runners-up included *Detecting Foreign Bodies in Food, The Aesthetics of the Japanese Lunchbox, Applications of High Tech Squids*, and *Sexual Health at Your Fingertips. Guardian, 21 Jan 2005.*

STRANGE DIETS

STEADY SALTED

Sports teacher Xiang Zhaocheng, 51, from Hunan province, China, baffled doctors because he seemed to suffer no ill effects from eating a pound (almost half a kilo) of salt every day. He carried it with him and swallowed a handful when he felt hungry. He appeared younger than many other people his age. *Hong Kong Standard, 24 Jan 1997.*

LIZARD LUNCH

Sandeep Chatterjee, an 18-year-old "vagabond" from Sakchi in the Indian state of Jamshedpur, lived on lizards, snakes, and all sorts of insects washed down with petrol. Aged five, he began stealing petrol from vehicles and gulping it down. He said lizards were his favourite food. He also relished dog and cat meat, having a preference for kittens. He sometimes ate roti and rice just for variety. He didn't complain of any health problems. *Hindustan Times (New Delhi), 21 Mar 1998.*

DIET OF LIZARDS

Veera Raungsri, 42, a Thai landscaper who recently took his ninth wife, eats two or three live geckos (house lizards) every day, which made him more virile than his first eight wives could cope with. He had a liver ailment 20 years earlier and was told it was incurable, but a Cambodian man advised him to eat live lizards and after two weeks he was better. *Hong Kong Standard, 19 June 1999.*

BEEDI FOOD

An Indian woman claimed to have lived for 50 years on a diet of cigarette stubs. Khayarunnisa, 61, from the southern state of Tamil Nadu, got up early each day to collect and eat subs of beedis, the small Indian cigarettes rolled in a leaf. "My father was a heavy smoker and I ate whatever was left of the stubs he threw away," she said. "I lost my appetite for normal food long ago." Her doctor said: "She says she can sleep well only if she has had a beedi meal. I have given up trying to persuade her to eat anything else." *Metro North East, 8 April 2002.*

GRAZING BELGIAN

Jurgen Tersago from Aalst in Belgium was observed in Berlare crawling out of his car on his hands and knees, eating grass in a field and grunting like a pig. The police arrived and took him to hospital, where tests revealed he was over the drink-drive limit. In court, he told the judge: "I like eating grass, especially when I'm drunk. It tastes like spinach." He was fined £680 and banned from driving for 45 days. *Ananova, 24 Mar 2003.*

NOTHING BUT GRASS

Gangarum Gautam, 41, said he started eating grass secretly when he was seven, after hearing about a ruler who ate grass bread. He claimed he had eaten nothing but grass for the last five years. The poor casual labourer was allowed to "graze" in his local park in Kanpur, India. Doctors said he was in good health – but two wives had left him because of his bizarre diet. *Sun, 8 Feb 2007.*

REPTILE CURE

A Thai farmer who claimed to have swallowed up to 15 live lizards every day for the past 30 years says they had kept him free from stomach pains and boosted his sex drive. Suwan Meunlow, 48, began suffering stomach-aches aged 18. Doctors were unable to help, but a neighbour told him that eating a small house lizard called a *jin jok* would make him feel better. *Ananova, 23 June 2002.*

I'LL DRINK TO THAT

SUPER-SOZZLED

An unnamed middle-aged man picked up by police in Latvia had twice the blood-alcohol level seen as fatal and probably set a world record. He was unconscious but stable after a blood test showed 7.22 parts per million of alcohol. An average person would vomit at 1.2, lose consciousness at three and stop breathing at about four parts per million. There was no record of anyone having survived such a dose – even in Russia. *Guardian, 19 Dec 2003.*

WELL EQUIPPED

Following a car accident, it was found that Josip Galic, 69, from Kucetine in Bosnia, had four kidneys. "It explained why I could drink all my friends under the table, and never had a hangover," he said. After a routine check-up, his brother Ante discovered that he also had four kidneys. The extra kidneys were normal in size and fully functional. *Ananova, 24 Feb 2004.*

GOING IT SOME

A Lithuanian truck driver, pulled over by police for driving in the middle of a two-lane highway in Vilnius, registered 7.27 grams per litre of alcohol in his blood – 18 times the legal limit, and more than twice the level usually regarded as fatal. When stopped and breathalysed, Vidmantas Sungaila, 41, grinned throughout. He was fined and banned from driving for three years. *Guardian, 24 May; Independent on Sunday, 28 May 2006.*

YUM YUM!

ACQUIRED TASTE

Scientists at the Environment Assessment Centre in Okayama City, south of Tokyo, turned raw sewage into a protein-rich substance resembling beef in texture. The protein is mixed with soybean and doctored with food additives and a steak sauce.

Mitsuyuki Ikeda, a member of the processing team, agreed that "sewage has a slight image problem" and was unlikely to threaten the established fast-food chains, but it could have a future as livestock feed. *(Brisbane) Courier-Mail, 8 Oct; Guardian, 15 Oct 1993.*

RICH PICKINGS

Dr Friedrich Bischinger, an Austrian physician, claims that picking your nose and eating it was one of the best ways to stay healthy: dead bacteria in snot boosts the immune system. He said that parents should urge their children to take up nose-picking – but most hardly needed encouragement as the saline and nutrients in nasal mucus are a savoury delight. *Sydney Sun Herald, 4 April 2004.*

" Dishes included testicle pizza and battered or barbequed testicles "

SUMMER NOVELTIES

Japanese ice-cream makers have been testing taste boundaries with this summer's flavours, which include eel, shrimp, oyster, octopus, squid, ox-tongue, garlic, potato & lettuce, strawberry & spinach, soybean & kelp, cactus, and raw horse. The last-named "has a vanilla taste, but you can really get the flavour of the horsemeat if you bite into a piece," said Miona Yamashita, 23. *Scotsman, 15 July; Ananova, 23 July 2004.*

BATTLE OF THE BALLS

Chefs gathered for the World Testicle Cooking Championships in Savinac, Serbia, on 3 November. The contest was won by Belgrade cook Dejan Milovanovic with his dish of bull and boar's organs. Testicles (or "white kidneys") are a national delicacy. Next year, an exotic category will be included where chefs have to make a dish using camel and ostrich privates. *Metro, 4 Nov 2004.*

MAY CONTAIN NUTS

Serbian chef Ljubomir Erovic, 45, published an e-book, *The Testicle Cookbook: Cooking With Balls*, on the YUDU website. Dishes include testicle pizza and battered testicles, and barbequed testicles and giblets. The balls come from stallions, ostriches, bulls, pigs, and turkeys. Balls are a traditional delicacy in Serbia, regarded as an aphrodisiac. *Irish Examiner, 8 Oct 2008.*

Write Your Way To A New Career!

Writers Bureau Celebrates Twenty-one Years of Helping New Writers
by Nick Daws

Hazel McHaffie

Tim Skelton

When distance-learning pioneer Ernest Metcalfe founded The Writers Bureau in the late 1980s, he can hardly have dared hope that twenty-one years on it would be acknowledged as Britain's leading writing school. Yet so it proved, with thousands of Writers Bureau students seeing their work in print for the first time. And, for many of those who persevered with their writing, the dream of becoming a successful writer has turned into reality.

Students such as Tim Skelton. An engineer by profession, he had always harboured an ambition to write, and at the age of 40 signed up with The Writers Bureau. The decision changed his life: "My writing career took off exponentially. In 2005 I started appearing regularly in lifestyle and in-flight magazines. The following year I was commissioned by Bradt Travel Guides to write a guidebook to Luxembourg. And in the last year

"My writing career took off exponentially."

I've appeared in The Times and The Independent, and updated guidebooks for Fodor's, Thomas Cook, and the AA."

Another student who benefited was Hazel McHaffie. Hazel wanted to make her academic work in Medical Ethics more accessible to people, and decided to write the themes into novels. Following her Writers Bureau course, Hazel has had five novels published, and appeared at the Edinburgh International Book Festival in 2008. She also has her own website at www.hazelmchaffie.com.

Sometimes studying with The Writers Bureau takes students down new and unexpected paths. Patricia Holness originally enrolled on The Writers Bureau's Writing for Children course. However, she soon realised that what she was learning applied to other types of writing as well.

She is now a full-time writer, regularly selling short stories for both children and adults. She also has a monthly column in Devon Life.

These are just a selection from the inspirational true stories from students of The Writers Bureau. There's no reason why YOU couldn't be their next success story. With a 15-day free trial and money-back guarantee, there is nothing to lose and potentially a whole new career to gain! So why not visit their website at www.writersbureau.com or call on Freephone 0800 856 2008 for more information?

Chapter 9

WEIRD SEX

For some people, obscure objects
of desire are the only kind – like the
lumberjack who caught rabies from
having sex with a raccoon, or the
woman who cut off her dead husband's
penis and planned to pickle it...

PARAPHILIA

RECTAL RODENT

Devito Bistone got a live gerbil stuck in his ascending colon. Koko Rodriguez attempted to rescue the animal with a cardboard cylinder, then lit a match "to improve visibility". A methane combustion occurred. Sistone was treated for burns at Salt Lake General Hospital, Utah. Rodriguez suffered a singed moustache and a broken nose. The gerbil survived. *British Medical Journal, May 1996.*

WILD AT HEART

Lumberjack Peter King, 37, who caught rabies after having sex with a raccoon, denied animal cruelty charges in Jasper, Tennessee. He claimed the racoon was already dead. *Glasgow Eve. Times, 6 June 1996.*

WHOA NELLIE!

Kim Lee Chong, a 61-year-old chef, was jailed for 15 years for trying to have sex with an elephant. He was caught naked from the waist down, standing on a box behind the animal. The father of five claimed the beast was the reincarnation of his wife, Wey. She had died 28 years earlier, shortly before her 29th birthday. Chong told the court in Phuket, Thailand: "I recognised her immediately... by the naughty glint in her eyes." *Sun, 28 Jan 1998.*

MARROW ESCAPE

A policeman in Ogden, Utah, spotted a small car parked in a cul-de-sac in the Ogden City Cemetery, rocking on its wheels. Inside was a partially clothed man banging his head violently against the steering wheel and "doing unnatural things with several squash-like vegetables". He was cited for lewdness, but insisted he had done nothing wrong. *Ogden (UT) Standard-Examiner, 1 Mar 1998.*

BEANZ MEANZ FINEZ

A motorist stopped at a police check in Colchester, Essex, was found to be wearing Wellington boots filled with baked beans in tomato sauce. "It is an offence not to be in proper control of a car," said a police spokesman. "Wearing boots full of baked beans could cause the driver to be distracted and have an accident." The driver was released after a warning. *Times, D.Telegraph, 30 June 1998.*

GAGGING FOR IT

Residents in Brunssum, Holland, witnessed a woman being handcuffed, blindfolded, gagged, and bundled into a van by three men. The police were alerted and 22 officers, believing they were foiling a kidnap, tracked the van for 18 miles (30km) in a helicopter, squad cars and motorbikes. They finally blocked the road in Heerlen, and found that the 21-year-old woman was dressed in fishnet stockings and high heels. When they removed her gag, she screamed: "You stupid bastards! I've been trying to set this up for months. You've ruined it!" *Melbourne Age, 10 Mar 2005.*

SEXUAL SHENANIGANS

PHONEY

A sex-line caller who complained to trading standards watchdogs when he got a woman nagging her husband instead of a panting girl was disappointed. They said they couldn't take any action as the line was titled "Hear me moan". *D.Record, 16 Jan 1996.*

STUCK ON YOU

An Australian burglar broke into a woman's home and deliberately glued the side of his face to her foot. Cops were stuck for a motive. *(Scottish) Sunday Mail, 10 Aug 1997.*

RUSSIAN PIONEERS

The inaugural race in the new sport of inflatable sex doll rafting, featuring dolls of both sexes, was held near St Petersburg on the white-water section of the Vuoksa River. It was won by Alexander Korolev, although

" His blow-up sex doll had a puncture and sounded more like a cow than a woman "

whether he was carried along by Phoebe the Flexible or Hellcat Hanna is not recorded. *Independent on Sunday, 31 Aug 2003.*

JUST HANGING AROUND

A fashionable pastime in Florida's Keys in summer 2003 was dangling from meat hooks. The Coast Guard and local police were called on 12 July to a sandbar off Whale Harbor in Islamorada, where five young people had erected a bamboo tripod with meat hooks hanging from it. A young woman, her feet brushing the surface of the water, dangled from the frame, hooks embedded in her shoulders. A dangling young man said he was "just enjoying the afternoon". No laws were being broken. *New York Daily News, 19 July 2004.*

ECSTATIC MOO

Dan Vasile, 40, from Brasov, Transylvania, was awarded £600 after claiming a life-size blow-up sex doll he had purchased had a slow puncture and needed "blowing up every few minutes". It also didn't "moan with pleasure" as it was supposed to do. "It sounded more like a cow than a woman," he complained. Romanian trading standards investigated and the shop owner agreed to compensate him. *Sun, (Dublin) Metro, 1 Feb 2008.*

DILDO BOULEVARD

An unnamed Australian town where 30 sex toys were found lying in front of a house has renamed the street "Dildo Boulevard". Resident Laurelle Bates said: "It's a real mystery. We have no idea where they came from. They look used." Within hours, many had disappeared. "Some of the bigger ones are gone," she noted casually. *New York Post, 18 Feb 2009.*

KEEP IT DOWN

Caroline and Steve Cartwright of Washington, Tyne & Wear, were given an ASBO (Antisocial Behaviour Order) because they made so much noise during sex. Neighbours and the local postman complained about the howling, reaching 47 decibels, which went on for two or three hours, virtually every night. A neighbour said: "It sounds like they are both in considerable pain." In December, Mrs Cartwright, 48, pleaded guilty to three counts of breaching the ASBO, and was given an eight-week suspended sentence. *BBC News, 10 Nov, 15 Dec, 2009, 22 Jan 2010.*

MANHOOD MISHAPS

FREE WILLY

Following the death in a car crash of his best friend Paul Simone, 33, Henri Cousteau (also 33) of Marseilles, became the beneficiary of an unusual legacy: in his will, M Simone left his 24cm (9.75in) penis for transplantation. "I never had real sex," said the less well endowed M Cousteau. "Paul had hundreds of women. Now I could have the same success." Dream on, Henri. *Sun, 29 July; Guardian, 28 Oct 1997.*

SUCKER FOR PUNISHMENT

Gerald Naud, 35, was ordered by a judge in Edmonton, Canada, to stop asking women to kick him in the testicles. He was jailed for 13 months, ironically for "sexual assault". *Metro, 17 Aug 2004.*

GRAVE RUBBING

Pere Lachaise cemetery in Paris has sealed off the grave of Victor Noir, the journalist shot dead in 1870 at the age of 22. The monument shows Noir lying on his back with a distinct enlargement in the groin region. Legend has it that he was due to wed the day after he was killed, which accounts for his apparent erection. The bronze statue has long been regarded as an aid to fertility by women, whose attentions have rubbed the protuberance to a smooth shine. Officials were alarmed by the growing frequency of the caresses, which were increasingly intimate and no longer confined to women. *Mortuary Management, vol.92, #3, Feb 2005.*

LOVE IS BLIND

In a New York paternity suit, it emerged that a transsexual, called 'Mr J' in court, had been married for 17 years to a society heiress before she discovered her husband was a woman. Mr J had had hormone treatment and breasts removed before he met and married 20-year-old 'Mrs C' when he was 30. He concealed his true gender by using a homemade plaster of Paris penis for sex. Their two children were born through artificial insemination. *D.Mail, 16 May 2006.*

INTIMATE KEEPSAKE

Uta Schneider, 65, hacked off her dead husband's penis in Stuttgart hospital. As she tried to smuggle it out, wrapped in foil and hidden in a lunchbox next to gherkins, she was spotted by a nurse and arrested for mutilation. Uta was wed to Heinrich, 68, for 35 years. She told police his pecker "was his best asset and gave me so much pleasure. I wanted to pickle it for eternity – it's what he would have wanted". *Sun, 12 Sept 2006.*

STRANGE FRUIT

Police found the testicles of Thomas Dietrich, 32, hanging from a tree after his gay lover ripped them off and hurled them from a train in Germany. *News of the World, 27 Sept 2009.*

Chapter 10

TOUGH LUCK

We all think we've been unlucky
at certain times in our lives,
but the unfortunate individuals in
this chapter give the expression
'having a bad day' a whole new
meaning. If we weren't too busy
laughing, we'd probably cry.

MEDICAL DISASTERS

LOSING HIS MARBLES

A Dutchman about to be married went into hospital to be circumcised by professionals. He awoke to be told that he had been given a vasectomy because of a mix-up in patient cards. His reaction is unrecorded. *[R] 4 Sept 1992.*

EASY MISTAKE

A Brazilian farmer with earache ended up having a vasectomy at a clinic in Montes Claros, in the state of Minas Gerais, after mistakenly believing the doctor had called his name. Valdemar Lopes de Moraes, 39, entered the operating room when Aldemar Aparecido Rodrigues' name was called. He asked no questions when the doctor started preparing to operate. He later explained that he thought his ear inflammation had got down to his testicles. He didn't want the operation reversed. *[R] 21 Aug 2003.*

CRACK TEAM ARSE-ABOUT

A German pensioner was suing a hospital after she checked in for a leg operation and woke up to find she had been given a new anus. The surgeons responsible, at a hospital in Hochfranken, Bavaria, were suspended after admitting they mixed up her notes with those of a woman suffering from chronic incontinence. *MX News (Brisbane), 19 Mar 2008.*

POETIC JUSTICE

FIERY RETRIBUTION

Joyce Rowsell refused to cut short her public telephone conversation so that a man could make an emergency call to the fire brigade. When she arrived back at her flat in Dartmouth, Devon, she found it well ablaze. The Good Samaritan had been trying to summon firefighters to put it out. *Sunday Mirror, 20 Sept 1992.*

SAFETY FIRST

According to *Police* magazine, a suspicious-looking cardboard box was found outside a Territorial Army centre in Bristol. The TA called the police, who called an army disposal unit, which blew the box up – to find it full of leaflets on how to deal with suspicious-looking packages. *Independent, 20 Jan 1993.*

COUP BLIMEY

The star speaker of a British Council seminar entitled "How Can Democracy be Sustained?", Brigadier Julius Maada Bio of Sierra Leone, was unable to attend, as he had just overthrown his country's government in an army coup. His first decree: to cancel the forthcoming elections. *D.Telegraph, 19 Jan 1996.*

PREDICTABLE

Following a conference on food poisoning held by the Public Health Laboratory Service in Colindale, north London, 30 of the 78 delegates went down with the stomach bug *campylobacter*. It was thought they had been poisoned by their lunch. *Guardian, 3 April 2001.*

FREUDIAN SLIP

Chris McDonnell, 58, a physiotherapist from Canterbury, Kent, who concluded in research that slippery banana skins were a comic myth, went flying when he slipped on a banana outside a local supermarket. *(London) Eve. Standard, 23 April 2004.*

NO HIDING PLACE

Florin Carcu, 54, asked his boss for the day off on Friday 13th August and refused to leave his house to avoid bad luck. However, he was fatally stung by a rare species of wasp in his kitchen in Cluj, Romania. Doris Needham, 74, changed her house number from 13 to 11a after being burgled twice – then fell victim to an arson attack in Sinfin, Derby. *[AFP] 14 Aug; Sun, 16 Aug 2004.*

" His fall was broken when he landed on top of a parked decorator's van "

JAM LEADS TO JAM

A German truck driver lost control of his vehicle while trying to swat a wasp and spilt his 15-tonne load of strawberry jam jars on the A1 motor-way near Greven, western Germany. The road was closed for two hours to clear up the mess, causing a long traffic jam. Police said the crash "really started attracting wasps. There was jam all over the motorway." *[R] 17 Aug 2004.*

READ ALL ABOUT IT

When Californian businessman Jack Pacheco was arrested for drug pos-session, he was anxious his neighbours should not read about it. So he bought every copy of the *Chowchilla News* he could find. However, the paper, impressed by its sales figures, ordered a reprint, the story got out, and Mr Pacheco was news coast to coast. *Independent on Sunday, 6 Mar 2005.*

THOROUGHLY STUFFED

Petru Cioaba, from the eastern Romanian town of Focasany, bought identical necklaces for his wife and mistress, with their initials and a personal message engraved. However, he sent each the wrong necklace and soon received a call from his mistress telling him he was dumped and a message from his wife's lawyer saying she was filing for divorce. *Metro, 9 Mar 2005.*

HELP & SAFETY

An office floor collapsed under the weight of a boardroom table during a meeting of 21 health and safety officers to discuss evacuation procedures. They fell to the floor below and landed in a heap with the table on top of them. One woman suffered spinal injuries and was taken to hospital along with three others, two with broken ankles. The remaining 17 escaped with minor cuts and bruises. The incident occurred at a schools supply firm based in a former mill in Hyde, Greater Manchester. *Manchester Eve. News, 22 Feb 2006.*

BY THEIR OWN HAND

(UN)LUCKY

A 23-year-old man jumped 220ft (67m) off the San Francisco-Oakland Bay Bridge on Boxing Day 1995, landing yards from a psychiatrist in a rowing boat with a life jacket and cell phone. Dennis Tison saw the would-be suicide, tossed him his life jacket and called the police. *[AP] 28 Dec 1995.*

NO WAY OUT

A German factory worker failed in his 10th suicide attempt when he was discovered after swallowing 60 sleeping pills. Previous efforts included rat poison (he vomited it up), a gun to the head (it jammed), and a hairdryer in the bath (the fuse blew). *Guardian, 11 July 1996.*

SUICIDE THWARTED

Trying to end it all, a 45-year-old man leapt from a corridor outside his sixth-storey flat in Hong Kong, but he survived. His fall was broken when he landed on top of a parked decorator's van. *The Australian, 27 May 2005.*

A DAY TO REMEMBER

A wedding reception in Iasi, Romania, turned sour when heartbroken

Anna Bratianu, 22 – in love with the groom – drank acid. As she writhed in agony, her best friend slashed her wrists in sympathy. Another guest then broke his toe on the dance floor and a 41-year-old woman smashed her shin while showing off disco moves. Finally, 26 guests went down with food and alcohol poisoning and filled every available bed in the local hospital. *Sun, 9 Oct 2008.*

JUST NOT THEIR DAY

WRONG BANGOR

Pop star Lena Fiagbe turned up for the Radio One Roadshow in Bangor. She wandered confused round the North Wales town while the live radio party was in full swing in Bangor, Northern Ireland. What really peeved her was that she had come from Ireland the day before. Thus she lost her chance to sing her smash hit – entitled 'Got To Get It Right'. *Western Mail, 22 July 1994.*

SHORT-LIVED

Three hundred tons of sand put down to make a new bathing beach at Burnham-on-Crouch, Essex, disappeared when the tide went out. *D.Telegraph, 28 Oct 1994.*

OH BROTHER!

A man from Barrow in Cumbria, who had lived in Australia for 30 years, returned to Cumbria in search of his long-lost brother, only to discover that he had emigrated – to Australia. *Cumbrian Sunday News and Star, 3 Sept 1995.*

POSTSCRIPT ERROR

A *Sunday Times* sub editor spent many years researching and writing a book called *The History of the Royal Mail*. The nameless sub is not believed to have savoured the irony when the only copy of the manu-script was lost in the post. *Guardian, 13 May 1997.*

LOVE'S BLIND

A Saudi woman who donated an eye to restore her husband's sight ended up losing him to another woman. The newspaper *Al-Jazirah* said the man couldn't stand the sight of his wife being one-eyed and decided to remarry. *[AFP] 16 June 1997.*

IN A PADDY

A meal in a remote Vietnamese mountain village got out of control when a four-year-old's fight over a barbecued locust ended with 19 houses burned to the ground. Some 18 tons of rice paddy was ruined and two classrooms razed in the incident. *[R] 22 Nov 1997.*

LOSING HIS DEPOSIT

A 61-year-old German who withdrew his life savings of 100,000 marks (£35,000) so that he could put the money in a higher interest account lost it all when he drove off, forgetting that the money was still on the roof of his car in the southern town of Balingen. *[R] 23 Dec 1998.*

STAN'S THE MAN

Three Hell's Angels are suing their tattooist after he misread their instructions and needled in "Stan's Slave" rather than "Satan's Slave". *Times, 4 Aug 1999.*

BUCKET-HEADED

Police arrested a naked Los Angeles woman wandering the street with a bucket over her head. She said she had stepped out onto her balcony and accidentally locked the door behind her. So she put the bucket on her head to hide her identity as she went for help – and got lost. *(Scottish) Sunday Mail, 12 Sept 1999.*

PERILS OF CHRISTIANITY

A woman who stopped at traffic lights in Detroit noticed a bumper sticker on the car in front of her that read "Honk if you love Jesus". So she did. The driver of the car in front then got out and bashed a dent in her bonnet with a baseball bat. *Sunday Times, 22 Oct 2000.*

OUT TO REGAIN ASHES

Donna Bello travelled the world to scatter her mother's ashes at places that were special to her – Vermont, Bali and Hawaii. Returning home, she discovered the Florida funeral home had given her the wrong ashes. She was suing. *Independent on Sunday, 3 Feb 2002.*

FOSSIL STOMPED

South African palæontologist Theagarten Lingham-Soliar found a rare metre-wide footprint of a giant brachiosaur in fossilised mud in Zimbabwe and went off to collect the latex he needed to cast a mould of the track. By the time he got back, a herd of elephants had obliterated it. *New Scientist, 26 June 2004.*

STIFF DRINK NEEDED

David Atkinson spent 18 years designing an experiment for Huygens, the unmanned European space mission to Saturn, which was launched from Cape Canaveral, Florida, in 1997. His purpose was to measure the winds on Titan, Saturn's largest moon. On 14 January 2005, Atkinson and his team were waiting for the data to arrive at the European Space Agency HQ in Darmstadt, Germany, when it was discovered that someone had forgotten to turn on his measuring instrument before takeoff. *[AP] 20 Jan 2005.*

TRAPPED BY BEACH BALLS

Following a swim in the sea off Valalta, western Croatia, Mario Visnjic relaxed in his beach deckchair, but later found his testicles were trapped between the wooden slats. They had shrunk while he had been skinny-dipping, but resumed normal volume in the sunshine. He called for help on his mobile, and a beach attendant cut the chair in half to release him. *Sunday Times, 6 Aug 2006.*

PAIN IN THE NECK

A man with no arms caught rabies after being bitten by a weasel that ran up his trousers and latched on to his neck. Aurel Constantinescu, 48, had to run for 15 minutes back to his home in Suceava, eastern

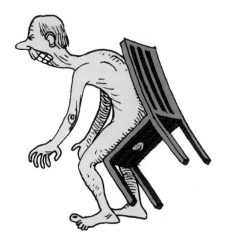

" He later found his testicles were trapped between the wooden slats "

Romania, where his wife pulled the animal off and killed it. *D.Record, 14 Sept 2007.*

IT'S PERSONAL

When a tornado hit Aurora, Missouri, on 8 January 2008, it shredded a few outhouses belonging to Ralph and Risby Atwood. It was the third tornado to target the Atwoods in five years. They lost everything to one in 2003 and again in March 2006. After this, they moved from just north of Aurora, southwards to a point near Crane, to get out of the tornadoes' paths; but there was no escape. "Forty years and there hasn't been a tornado here," said Ralph. "Then we moved here. It's like I got a magnet in my back." *YouNewsTV, 11 Jan 2008.*

TROUSER KINDLING

A Polish cyclist received second-degree burns after apparently pedalling so hard his trousers caught fire. Mieczyslaw Jasinski, 55, leapt from his bike and rolled on the ground when he smelled burning as he rode home in Koroszczyn. "Witnesses said he was like a human torch cycling along," said police. *Metro, 28 Feb 2008.*

BAD TIMING

Melchiorre Contena, a Sardinian pastor, spent 30 years in jail for the kidnap and murder of an Italian businessman, continually protesting his innocence. In 2007, the real killers were caught and a judge ordered Contena's release – which came 12 hours before his sentence was to end and he would have been released anyway. *(Dublin) Metro, 19 Nov 2008.*

MARRIAGE OF MYSTERY

A Saudi Arabian woman wants a divorce after her husband sneaked a look at her face after 30 years of marriage. The 50-year-old followed the tradition of her native village near the south-western city of Khamis Mushayt and kept her features hidden at all times – but one night in April 2008 her husband lifted her veil as she slept to take a look, and she woke up. He apologised and promised never to do it again, but the damage was done. The custom of hiding the face from everyone is observed by a tiny minority of women in remote areas of Gulf countries. *D.Mail, 19 May 2008.*

WITH DEEP REGRET

On 29 January 2008, Robert Napier, 67, took to London for valuation the violin he and his siblings had inherited from their mother. Made in 1698 by Matteo Goffriller in Venice, it was valued at £180,000. Returning by train, he alighted at his stop – Bedwyn in Wiltshire – but as the train drew away he realised the violin was still on the luggage rack. The train was searched at Taunton, but the precious instrument had gone. *D.Telegraph, D.Mail, 15 April 2008.*

THOROUGHLY FLEECED

Attila Miklos, 27, had his wallet stolen by a masked man with a gun at the railway station in Kaposvar, Hungary. As he walked to the police station to report the incident, the same man jumped out of some bushes and took his watch and mobile, shouting: "I forgot to take these!" Finally, just yards from the police station, a car drove up and the same robber got out and took his laptop. *(Dublin) Metro, 22 May 2008.*

Chapter 11

FOR THE BIRDS

Our feathered friends constantly
surprise us with their behaviour,
whether it's the thieving crow
that targeted cash machines,
the foul-mouthed parrot that nearly
embarrassed the Queen or the stork
that stalked a pair of Germans.

BIRD TALK

BETRAYED BY A PARROT

Bozo, a cockatoo belonging to Carlos and Rosella DeGambo, was called to testify at their divorce hearing in Argentina. Lawyers showed the bird a picture of a young woman who supposedly visited the apartment. "Honeybun, I love you!" shrieked Bozo. Asked "Who loves Carlos?" Bozo replied: "Ruby loves Carlos. Ruby loves her baby." (Ruby was Mr DeGambo's secretary.) Despite objections, the civil court judge allowed Bozo's testimony to stand and granted the divorce. *Toronto Sun, 9 Mar 1990.*

MYNAH OFFENCES

Friedrich Baier, 46, a sex pest from Cologne, harassed many women on the phone while posing as a doctor. The law caught up with him when his pet mynah bird screeched out his owner's name and the woman on the line told the police. *D.Express, 25 July 1998.*

GIVE US A CLUE

Trading standards officers looking for pirate computer games found counterfeit disks and copying equipment at a house in Mountain Ash, South Wales, but were unable to find the master disks until the owner's parrot squarked: "Under the mattress! Under the mattress!" They uncovered two cases containing 200 games, worth about £10,000. *D.Telegraph, D.Mail, 11 Sept 1998.*

PARROT CLUES

A woman from Chongqing in China had her suspicions about her husband's infidelity confirmed by their mynah bird, according to the *Xinmin Evening News.* After the woman returned from a month's visit to her parents, the bird said things like "divorce", "be patient", and "I love you", particularly when the telephone rang. Seeking a divorce, the woman brought the bird to a lawyer for a consultation, hoping it could testify in court, but he told her not to build up her hopes. *[R] 20 June 2001.*

PARROT BREAKS SILENCE

A retired policeman went out of his Kiev flat, leaving his parrot alone. When he returned after a few minutes, he found three would-be thieves stretched out on the floor with their hands behind their heads. They explained that when they came into the flat, they heard a voice say: "Stop! I'll shoot! On the ground!" The parrot, which had lived with the policeman for a year, had never spoken before the incident. All this according to the *Cegodnya* newspaper. *Ananova, 7 Oct 2003.*

ANOTHER FINE MESS

Eight stolen cockatiels got themselves rescued by whistling the Laurel and Hardy theme tune. A man heard the tune coming from a house in Salisbury, Wiltshire, and told police, who raided the property. The unnamed owner said his collection of 30 cockatiels all liked to whistle the tune. *Sun, 21 Feb 2004.*

PROVOCATIVE PARROT

Li Yong, from Zhengzhou in the Chinese province of Henan, strangled his parrot because it kept calling him names. He spent eight months trying to teach the bird to say "hello" and "goodbye" but it refused to speak. He eventually lost his temper and called the bird "idiot" and other names and the parrot then repaid him by repeating the insults every time he passed. *[DPA] Sydney Morning Herald, 3 Feb 2004.*

FOUL-BEAKED

Sunny, an African grey parrot aboard *HMS Lancaster*, was initially ordered ashore to avoid embarrassing the Queen during a royal visit to Portsmouth on 5 March, but won a last-minute reprieve.

The ship's avian mascot shouts "Arse!" at members of the crew, "Fuck off!" at top brass, and "Show us your tits!" when women pass. She also says "Bollocks!", "You ain't seen me, right?" and "Zulus, thousands of 'em!" What's more, she can whistle the theme tune to *The Great Escape. D.Telegraph, 3 Mar; Sun, 3+4 Mar; Sunday Times, 7 Mar 2004.*

" The obsessed bird even tapped on their bedroom window if they stayed indoors "

PARROT NOT SICK

Marilyn King of Cumbernauld, Scotland, was worried when Nelson, her 13-year-old parrot, started wheezing, apparently struggling for breath, muttering, groaning and calling for help, but medical tests could find nothing wrong. She then discovered that Nelson had previously lived in an old people's home and was mimicking the sounds he had heard there. "He has a whole repertoire of coughing," said Ms King, "but his smoker's cough is the best." *D.Mail, 26 Feb 2005.*

POLLY PHONIC

Stuart McNae, 54, from Huddersfield, West Yorkshire, has had to change his mobile phone ringtone five times because his parrot keeps copying them. Billy, a blue-fronted Amazon, waits until he leaves the room, mimics the sound of a call, then laughs when he dashes back to answer. He has gone through the Nokia theme, Lou Bega's Mambo Number 5, the Match of the Day tune, Soul Mambo by Booker T and the MGs, and Bob Marley's No Woman No Cry. *Sun, 7 Dec 2007.*

POLLY BAD LUCK

Hayley Wilson bought a talking parrot for £440 in Crediton, Devon – and found it could speak only Polish. *Sunday Mirror, 9 Mar 2008.*

BIRD BRAIN

Mr Jiang of Nanjing, China, bought a mynah bird and taught it to speak in order to attract customers. He then bought two parrots, but their constant chattering annoyed the mynah, which jumped about frenetically. The mynah then noticed that when a neighbouring cat came and miaowed, the parrots fell silent. So it began to imitate the miaow, and peace was restored. *North-West Eve. Mail, 22 Sept 2008.*

BAD BIRDS

IN A FLAP

Lynn Jones, 27, noticed her underwear was going missing off her washing line in Ashburton, Devon, and suspected a pervert. However, when a dangerous tree was felled in her garden, the garments turned up in a crow's nest. *News of the World, 20 Sept 1988.*

AIRBORNE HEIST

A crow snatched half a million lire (£160) from a man withdrawing money from a cash machine in Sicily. As the bank notes emerged from the machine in Pace del Mela village near Messina, the bird swooped onto the 40-year-old accountant and snatched the bills from the tray. Police thought the bird was trained to steal and reported that a man with a pet crow had recently been seen in the area. *Metro, 24 Jan; Houston Chronicle, 29 Jan 2001.*

STALKING STORK

A German couple claimed a stork had been following them for weeks. The obsessed bird even tapped on their bedroom window if they stayed indoors. "It's a nightmare," said Gerhard Schneider, 72, of Brandenburg an der Havel. "He either knocks on the window or is sitting on my car waiting for us. My car has been scratched and we can barely leave the house." *Metro, 23 May 2006.*

THIEVING BIRDS

Mandy Spencer, 70, found an injured seagull on the beach near her home in Penzance, Cornwall. After nursing it back to health for two months, she released it. Days later, it returned looking for food, saw her false teeth in a glass in the kitchen, and flew away with them.

Law student Sam Rozati, 23, was walking past a lake on Essex University campus when he was set upon by three geese. He dropped his phone and one of the birds ran off with it in its beak. *Sunday Mirror, 13 May; Metro, 15 May 2007.*

CADGING COFFEE

A woman in Snappertuna, southern Finland, was on a coffee break when a raven joined her. "It landed on the table and took the spoon from my cup," she said. "Then it put the spoon down, stuck its beak into the cup and began gulping down coffee." The raven stayed the whole afternoon and was treated to cheese and cat food. Neighbours knew of the bird, which had a habit of trying (unsuccessfully) to steal mobile phones. *Västra Nyland (Finland), 31 July 2007.*

SNATCHED BY EAGLE

Keira-Jane Keegan, 23, was playing with her kitten Lacy in her Sydney garden when a sea eagle swooped down, gripped the kitten's head in its talons, and flew off. The bird dropped the 10-week-old kitten about a kilometre away in another garden. The couple that lived there took her to an RSPCA centre, where her head wounds were stitched up and she was given antibiotics. Miss Keegan's calls to animal shelters and the Government Pet Line finally saw kitten and owner reunited. *(Sydney) D.Telegraph, 14 April; D.Mail, 16 April 2007.*

BIRD BRAINS

CROW FOR HIM

Police in Kvam, near Bergen in Norway, searched for 10 days for the body of a 17-year-old boy whose motorcycle had crashed. They suspected he had been thrown into a waterfall, which they searched with divers, camera and dogs. Finally, testing a folk belief that roosters can find drowned people, the sheriff and a colleague rowed out on the lake with a rooster in a tightly shut cardboard box. After a few hundred feet, the bird started crowing and the body was found nearby. *Western Mail, 3 Sept 1998.*

GOLDEN WINDFALL

After a strong north-easterly gale, a kestrel suffering from a broken wing and dehydration was brought in to a rehabilitation centre in Seahouses, Yorkshire. It was found to be grasping a Danish coin in its talons. Had it brought the coin all the way from Scandinavia? If so, why? Graham Bell, who runs the centre, thought the bird brought the coin as payment for board and lodging. *New Scientist, 12 Dec 1998.*

SAVED BY SWAN

When a bear jumped into a lake at Kyyjarvi, 250 miles (400km) north of Helsinki, and chased two fishermen in a rowing boat, they called for help on their mobile phones. But a swan appeared above them and attacked the swimming bear, pecking at its head until it left. *Newcastle Journal, 17 June 1999.*

FOWL S.O.S.

Two chickens escaped from a laying shed at a Norfolk farm at 8am on 10 September. They then knocked the receiver off a telephone 4ft (1.2m) up a wall and managed to dial 999. When control room staff at Norfolk police could get no response from the call, they sent officers racing to the poultry unit at Hill Farm, South Raynham, near Fakenham – to be met by embarrassed farm operatives. "It is a one-in-a-million chance they hit three nines," said hatchery manager Derek Frost. *Eastern Daily Press, 11 Sept 1999.*

SEAGULL SCORES

In a football match between Stalybridge Celtic Colts and Hollingworth Juniors in Dukinfield, Greater Manchester, a Stalybridge attack culminated in a 25-yard volley that was heading way over the crossbar until a seagull swooped down and headed the ball into the net. After a few seconds it regained its equilibrium and flew away. "If the ball does not go out of the pitch area, it can't be disallowed," said Damian Whelan, the referee. "Even a dog can score a goal." An FA spokesman agreed. *D.Mail, 1 Oct; Irish Independent, 4 Oct 1999.*

FEARLESS FOWL

Bev Robson of Bexhill, East Sussex, was stunned by one her chickens, dubbed Snowy the wonderhen. The bird could scale obstacles, race up and down ladders and even walk a tightrope. One day she jumped up on the family pony and started riding around. *Metro, 12 Jan 2004.*

BIRD OF HABIT

A blackbird surprised experts by flying 240 miles (386km) to the same garden on the same day two years running. The bird was ringed in Thetford, Norfolk, before flying to Robin Woods's garden in Newton Abbot, Devon, on Boxing Day 2003. The next spring, she went back to her original garden before appearing back in Mr Woods's garden on Boxing Day 2004. "Blackbirds rarely travel, but this one is different," said an ornithologist. *D.Mail, 18 Jan 2005.*

COCK BOXING

The Oklahoma legislature banned cock fighting in 2002, but a local politician is trying to achieve its comeback with a plan that he believes will satisfy animal rights campaigners. Rather than having razors strapped to the cocks' heels, Senator Frank Shurden wants them to wear boxing gloves and vests with electronic sensors to record hits and keep score. *Brisbane Courier-Mail, 28 Jan; Guardian, 29 Jan 2005.*

RECORD EGG

The largest hen's egg ever recorded was laid in Jiaozuo, China, on 18 March 2005. It was 8.5cm (3.3in) long, 6.1cm (2.4in) wide and weighed 206g (7.3oz). Although it beat the heaviest egg in the *Guinness Book of Records* – 148g (5.2oz), laid in Ukraine in February 2004 – Chen Xiaobai, the eight-month-old hen's owner, did not say whether she would apply for a place in the record book. *Indo-Asian News Service, 24 Mar 2005.*

**" The largest
hen's egg ever
recorded was
3.3 inches long
and 2.4 inches
wide "**

PARROT TRICKS

African Grey parrot Tommy was given the boot by two owners in Newton
Abbott, Devon, because of his deafening impressions of someone snor-
ing. A month later, Peter Taylor of Mirfield, Yorkshire, had taken out his
hearing aids and was asleep when fire broke out. His life was saved by
his African Grey parrot Merlin, who mimicked the sound of the smoke
alarm and ran up and down his legs. *Sun, 16 Feb; Canberra Times, 26
Mar 2006.*

SURPRISE STASH

A crow dropped six rings, two bracelets and four necklaces worth £243
into a sock on Ron Page's washing line in Nether Wallop, Hampshire.
Sun, 12 Mar 2007.

PARROTMEDIC

Charlie the parrot was flying free when his owner had a heart attack. As
Jeff Blunt, 45, passed out, Charlie landed on the phone, knocked off
the receiver and hit the redial button. That sent a call to Jeff's friend
John Radcliffe, who recognised the caller's number but could only just
make out the sound of Jeff groaning in agony. He dashed round, used a
spare key to get in and called an ambulance, saving his friend's life. *The
People, 30 Dec 2007.*

A Startling Memory Feat That YOU Can Do!

How I learned the secret in one evening. It has helped me every day."

When my old friend Richard Faulkner invited me to a dinner party at his house, I little thought it would be the direct means of doubling my salary in less than two years. Yet it was, and here is the way it all came about.

Towards the end of the evening things began to drag a bit as they often do at parties. Finally someone suggested the old idea of having everyone do a 'party-piece'. Some sang, others forced weird sounds out of the

piano, recited, told stories and so on.

Then it came to Peter Brown's turn. He said he had a simple 'trick' which he hoped we would like. First he asked to be blindfolded. Those present were to call out 25 random numbers of three figures each, such as 161, 249, and so on. He asked me to list the numbers in order as they were called.

Peter then astounded everyone by repeating the entire list of 25 numbers backwards and forwards. Then he asked people to request numbers by their position in the list, such as the eighth number called, the fourth number and so on. Instantly he repeated back the correct number in the positions called. He did this with the entire list – over and over again without making a single mistake.

Then Peter asked someone to

shuffle a deck of cards and call them out in order. Still blindfolded he instantly named the cards in their order backwards and forwards.

You may well imagine our amazement at Peter's remarkable memory feat.

"There was really nothing to it – simply a memory feat"

On the way home that evening I asked Peter Brown how it was done. He said there was really nothing to it — simply a memory feat. Anyone could develop a good memory, he said, by following a few simple rules. And then he told me exactly how to do it.

What Peter said I took to heart. In one evening I made remarkable strides towards improving my memory. In just a few days I learned to do exactly what he had done.

"I can instantly recall anything I want to remember"

I was fast acquiring that mental grasp and alertness I had so often admired in men who were spoken of as "brilliant" and "geniuses".

Then I noticed a marked improvement in my writing and conversational powers. What's more my salary has increased - dramatically.

These are only a few of the hundreds of ways I have profited by my trained memory. Now I find it easy to recall everything I read. I can recall in

detail almost at will. I rarely make a mistake.

What Peter told me that eventful evening was this: "Send for details of Dr. Bruno Furst's Memory Course." I did. That was my first step in learning to do all the remarkable things I have told you about. In fact, I was so impressed that I got permission to publish Dr. Furst's Course myself.

BOB HEAP

We, the publishers, have printed full details of Dr. Furst's unique memory training method in a free information pack. For your free copy, either phone **0800 298 7070** free, post the coupon below, visit our website at **www.firstclassmemory.com** or send an e-mail (see coupon) **TODAY**.

Chapter 12

LOST AND FOUND

A doll left on a rubbish tip is stuffed
with diamonds, recycling from Leeds
is found in India, a dead horse is
discovered jammed in a ventilation
shaft 12 storeys up, and the world's
biggest dinosaur turd - you never know
what will turn up.

DIAMONDS!

WHAT GOES AROUND

Barry Stroop was hoeing his carrots in Xenia, Ohio, on 21 July 1991 when he found a man's gold diamond ring. Recalling that his friend Woody Lott had lost such a ring, he visited Lott that evening, who recognised the ring as a family heirloom. He had lost it on his mother's farm in 1985. Twice a year, Lott carted manure six miles (10km) to Stroop's garden. He guessed that a cow had eaten the ring and passed it in a load of manure. *Philadelphia (PA) Enquirer, 29 July 1991.*

RING MY BELL(Y)

Surgeons operating on 67-year-old Janet Webb's 'tumour' in Cedar Rapids, Iowa, found a diamond ring lost 44 years earlier during a Caesarean operation. The same thing happened to Virginia Argue in Roseville, California, six months earlier. She had carried a diamond ring in her stomach for 50 years. *D.Record, 1 Feb 1994; (Scottish) Sunday Mail, 11 July 1993.*

DIAMOND TOOTH LIL

Liliana Parodi didn't have to pay for her pasta in her favourite restaurant in Genoa, Italy, after a small stone wedged in one of her teeth. The next day the stone was removed and turned out to be an uncut diamond worth almost £2,000. *D.Record, D.Mirror, 26 April 1996.*

LITTLE GEM

Five-year-old Nicole Ohlsen of Bachum in Germany found a doll on a rubbish tip. After she took it home, her mother Ute was about to throw it out when she discovered £45,000 worth of diamonds hidden inside. Police told the family they could keep the gems, which were to be used to pay for Nicole's education. *Weekly News, 27 July 1996.*

FAR FROM HOME

BIN AND GONE

Aidan Pedreschi, from Dublin, on a charity cycle ride around the world, made an odd discovery on leaving a hotel in the obscure Romanian town of Lovrin. Every wheelie bin in the place was branded with the name of Fingal County Council – his local authority back in Dublin, some 1,250 miles (2,000km) away. A spokesman for Fingal said the authority didn't sell old bins to anyone. *Northside People (Dublin), 15 Oct 2008.*

FAR-FLUNG

Rubbish put out for recycling in Leeds ended up being dumped in India. Environmental campaigners found junk mail sent to Paul Sharman's home in disused wells in the state of Tamil Nadu. Leeds City Council denied sending any recycling material to India. *MX News (Brisbane), 16 Oct 2008.*

SUITCASE MYSTERY

The Bennett family flew from Southampton to Paris for Christmas, but one of their suitcases failed to arrive with them. Air France said it had "vanished". It was later found in the city of Farah in Afghanistan and was returned to Southampton airport within a week. There are no flights to Afghanistan from either Southampton or Paris's Charles de Gaulle airport, so how the case reached Farah is unknown. *BBC News, 1 Jan 2009.*

ANTIQUITIES

COIN FROM THE DEEP

Tony Framingham reeled in a 16lb (7.2kg) cod a mile off Dovercourt in Essex and found in its belly a Roman coin dating from the reign of Emperor Septimus Severus, around AD 200. *Sun, D.Star, 15 June 1994.*

" The 75-million-year-old fossil is the world's largest dinosaur dropping "

HORNING IN

A team of archæologists from Yogyakarta's Gadjah Mada University in Indonesia were reported to be examining the fossil of a horned man they had found in the Lembata Island village of Kadang. Johanes Kia, head of the tourist office, said that the expedition was "part of the local government's scientific efforts to discover more tourist objects". *Jakarta Post, 3 Jan 1998.*

FEARSOME FLOTSAM

In 2001, an antique carved ironwood war club used by cannibals from the Marquesas Islands in the South Pacific washed up in Swansea Bay, South Wales, 16,000 miles (26,000km) away. *(London) Eve. Standard, 4 April 2001.*

CHAMPION TURD

A fossil found near Onefour in southeastern Alberta was identified as the world's largest dinosaur dropping. The 75-million-year-old coprolite was about the size of a kitchen stove and contained well-preserved dinosaur muscle tissue, which is extremely rare. A paper on the find was published in the scientific journal *Palaios*. *[UPI] 7 Sept 2003.*

BRONZE AGE FIND

Archæologists spotted a gold necklace dating back to 3,000 BC on the neck of a woman working in a Bulgarian grocery store. The cashier's husband, Boris Todorov, 43, dug up gold rings on his farm and strung them together for his wife to wear. This tale echoes that of archæologist James Mellaart, who claimed to have encountered a girl wearing a Bronze Age gold bracelet on a Turkish train in 1958, allegedly leading him to the "Royal Treasure of Dorak". *The London Paper, 2 Aug 2007.*

FANTASTIC FINDS

BOTANIST'S BOTTOMS

Botanists from New Zealand's conservation department had spent years searching for *Corybas carseii*, an orchid feared extinct. After four days in a peat bog in search of the tiny native plant, which flowered only two days a year, the demoralised botanists paused for a lunch break and found they were sitting on one. There were 14 other specimens nearby. *[R] 2 Oct 1991.*

DITCHING THE FINGERS

Police called off a murder inquiry launched after two fingers were discovered by the side of State Highway One near Auckland, New Zealand, on 16 February 2001. It was discovered that the amputated fingers belonged to a man who kept them in a jar in his car, but forgot about them when he sold the car. When the new owners discovered the fingers, they threw them out of the window. *TNT Magazine, 19 Feb; Sunday Times, 25 Feb 2001.*

WHITE SALE

A German woman who bought a suitcase at an auction of unclaimed airline luggage tried to do her laundry with the contents of a washing powder carton she found in the case. It was in fact more than 4lb (1.8kg) of heroin, said the Frankfurt police. *Guardian, 18 Oct 1991.*

BUTTERED SHOES

A Swedish couple hiking on a remote mountain in Sweden's far northern province of Jaemtland found 70 pairs of shoes, all filled with half a kilo (1lb) of butter. There were trainers, high heels, boots and tap shoes. The find was similar to a display arranged by artist Yu Xiuzhen in 1996. His exhibit "Shoes With Butter," was laid out in the Tibetan mountains surrounding Lhasa. We were not told if Yu had visited Sweden. *[AP] 9 Oct 2003.*

WEIRD FLY-TIPPING

Shortly after Jason and Claire Foster moved into an isolated farmhouse in Ludford, near Market Rasen in Lincolnshire, an old pair of shoes appeared at the end of their drive. In the following five months, 30 pairs of footwear appeared on Sunday mornings, ranging from toddlers' sandals to expensive designer brands and roller-blades, some worn, others brand new with price tags and shoetrees. Covert video surveillance showed an elderly couple in a green vehicle tossing a collection of shoes. Following publicity, deliveries ceased and the Fosters auctioned the collection for charity. *BBC News, 14+29 Mar; D.Mail, 15 Mar 2005.*

HIGH HORSE

Police called to investigate an horrendous stench in a block of flats in Prokuplje, southern Serbia, ordered the building to be evacuated because of fears the overpowering fumes could be lethal. They then found the putrefying remains of a dead horse jammed into a ventilation shaft 12 storeys up. How it got there and why was a mystery. *Ananova, 22 Sept 2008.*

WALLET FULL OF TEETH

A Wal-Mart customer in Falmouth, Massachusetts, found 10 human teeth when he unzipped a compartment in a wallet he was about to buy on 28 February 2009. One tooth had a filling. He handed the wallet to employees and left without giving his name. Police said they were unable to perform DNA tests, as there was no blood or gum tissue on the teeth. *Cape Cod (MA) Times, 3 Mar 2009.*

Chapter 13

BIZARRE BELIEFS

People believe the strangest things, for all sorts of reasons. Can running around naked shouting at trees save your marriage? Could your husband be transformed into a hippo? Is drinking rat pee really good for the sex drive?

NOW YOU SEE IT...

BEARLY CREDIBLE

A crowd of about 50 people spent most of the night at Norman Gordon's farm in Keithville, Tennessee, on 6 February 1991 as Sheriff's deputies, game wardens and wildlife biologists tried to rescue a black bear caught 60ft (18m) up a pine tree. A vet fired tranquillizer darts at the critter in an unsuccessful effort to get it down, while a net was held underneath. It wasn't until the tree was felled the next morning that the "bear" was found to be a black bin liner. *[AP] 9 Feb 1991.*

OUT OF SEASON

On Christmas Day 1994, Niyi Owoeye was driving his bus near Akure, capital of Nigeria's Ondo state, when he thought he saw an antelope by the side of the road. Fancying a snack, he drove at it and crushed it. Then he discovered that it was really Mr Ratimi Alesanmi, a member of the Federal Commission for Road Safety. *Ivoir'Soir (Ivory Coast), 29 Dec 1994.*

SNUFF MOVIE

People coming to see the film *Deadly Virus* in a Berlin cinema stepped over a dead usher's body in the darkened entrance, thinking he was a dummy promoting the movie. Some were even seen kicking him and walking on his back. Max Bauer had, in fact, suffered a fatal heart attack just before the film opened. *D.Star, 27 April 1995.*

PEEPING EMU

An hysterical woman rang police to report that a bare-chested man with two big white dots tattooed on his forehead had stared through her window in Hamburg. Officers believe it was an emu that had escaped from a zoo twice in two weeks, but were taking no chances. "We're looking for a naked man with huge eyes – or an emu," said a spokesman. *[R] 24 Aug 2002.*

ALIEN SCARE

People in the quiet Brazilian town of Aracruz saw a fireball falling to earth before finding a small, badly burnt body, which they assumed was an alien. Worried about extraterrestrial invasion, more than 50 people called the police, while the corpse was taken to a local hospital – where it was identified as a rubber doll. *Irish Examiner, 22 Mar 2005.*

TRANSFORMATIONS

THE BLIND LIAR

A resident of Jenin in occupied Palestine, driving one evening towards Mevo Dotan, picked up a hitchhiker. After a while he noticed that the face of his passenger had changed into that of a one-eyed dog. Stopping the car, he ran away and fainted after observing the strange figure depart. The event stirred much debate. Some mullahs said the creature was a demon, while others said it was "the blind liar", a figure supposed to be committing evil acts before the coming of the Messiah. *Daily Maariv (Israel), 14 Oct 1996.*

SHAPE-SHIFTER

Police in Nigeria freed a 75-year-old man detained after he was attacked by a crowd that claimed he had turned from a vulture into a human being. As the bird fell to the ground, it changed into a three-year-old boy and started ageing rapidly, reaching 75 years of age in a quarter-hour. *National Post (Toronto), 31 Aug 1999.*

WITH EARRINGS?

A strange birth was front-page news in the Congo for several days. Romain Makolo, a physician at the biomedical hospital in Kinshasa, allegedly discovered "something mysterious" on the ultrasound scan of the abdomen of a woman called Omba Och, who had fertility problems. She later gave birth to an eel with golden earrings. Not everyone believed the story. *Het Nieuwsblad (Belgium), 8-9 May 1999.*

" A woman in southern Iran was reported to have given birth to a baby resembling a frog "

HIPPO HUSBAND

Following the shooting of a rogue hippopotamus, a woman in the Mashonaland West town of Mhangura in Zimbabwe went into mourning, alleging that the hippo was her husband who had changed in order to look for food to satisfy his ancestors. The husband had not been seen since the animal was killed. The woman pointed out that a red cloth tied to the hippo's left leg was identical to the one that her husband always wore. The local police expressed doubt over the claim, on the strange grounds that "scores of residents had eaten the hippo's meat when it was distributed to them". *Herald (Harare), 30 Dec 1999.*

SURPRISE BIRTH

Tawa Ahmed, 30, from Ondo, Nigeria, shocked churchgoers by claiming her five-year pregnancy ended in the birth of a tortoise; the 2lb 2oz (1kg) reptile was snuggled up beside her. She gave birth after the pastor of the Rock of Ages Gospel Church, Olusegen Mayaki, organised a 14-day religious event to ease her labour pains. He admitted he had been "surprised" when he saw the tortoise. Doctors were hoping to examine the woman to verify her claims – or not. *Metro, 8 Dec 2000.*

REBORN AS LIZARD

Chamlong Taengnium, 51, whose 13-year-old son Charoen died in a motorcycle crash, said the 5ft (1.5m) monitor lizard that followed her home after her son's cremation on 17 June 2001 was his reincarnation and brought good fortune. The lizard slept on his mattress and loved his favourite beverage – fresh milk and drinking yoghurt. Crowds of up to 200 people were thronging outside the house in Nonthaburi, 20 miles (32km) north of Bangkok, offering their respects and showering the creature with gifts. Some hunted for lottery numbers on its skin. *[R] 29 June 2001.*

FROG BIRTH

A woman was reported to have given birth to a "so-called frog" in the south-eastern Iranian city of Iranshahr on 26 June 2004. It allegedly grew from a 'larva' that entered the mother-of-two as she swam in a dirty pool. Her periods stopped for six months and tests showed she had a cyst in her abdomen. The daily *Etemaad* quoted clinical biology expert Dr Aminifard as saying that the grey creature resembled a frog "in appearance, the shape of the fingers, and the size and shape of the tongue." *BBC News, 27 June; Metro, 29 June 2004.*

ROBBER GOAT

"Vigilantes saw some hoodlums attempting to rob a car," said a police spokesman in the eastern Nigerian state of Kwara. "One escaped, while the other turned into a goat. The goat is in our custody." He said the "armed robbery suspect" would remain in custody until investigations were over. The car was a Mazda 323 and the goat was black and white. *BBC News, 23 Jan; D.Mail, 24 Jan 2009.*

FROG WORSHIPPED

Villagers in southern India were worshipping a frog that constantly changed colour. It was discovered by Reji Kumar in Thiruvananthapuram, Kerala. At first it was white, but it soon changed to yellow and then grey. "By night the frog was dark yellow," he said, "and then it became transparent so you could see its internal organs." Zoology professor Oommen V Oommen from Kerala University said he hoped to collect the unusual frog for study, but Kumar was worried it would croak first, as it was refusing all the food he offered. *D.Telegraph, 8 June 2009.*

BAD COUNSEL

BRAINWAVE

A Chinese farmer was arrested for stealing the head of a dead teenager and feeding the brains to his wife in an attempt to cure her of epilepsy. The man got the idea from an itinerant quack visiting his village in Yiliang county, Yunnan province. He was arrested before completing the cure ordained by the quack. *[AFP] 11 July 2002.*

FOLK FOLLY

Yang Qunying, 50, mistakenly believed the folk prescription that drinking rat urine would nourish her kidneys and help increase her sexual urge. She set some bait in her pigsty, guided the female rat to excrete in a bowl, and collected urine. But her breasts became swollen and she was diagnosed with cyclomastopathy at a hospital in Chongqing two weeks later, after she had breathing difficulties. *Ananova, 11 May 2004.*

NICER COOKED?

A Chinese man, identified only as Chen, went to an alternative medicine expert in Hunan province because of severe neck pains. He was told to eat at least six raw frogs a day and had scoffed his way through 130 before he collapsed, complaining of stomach pains and headaches. He sued the medicine man after doctors discovered his body was riddled with parasites from the frogs. *Ananova, 24 May 2004.*

TREE THERAPY

A husband was arrested for following his marriage guidance counsellor's advice: to run around naked shouting at trees. Dieter Braun, 43, said the tree relief was effective and stopped him shouting at his wife; the police, however, charged him with causing a public nuisance. *Metro, 12 July 2005.*

MELLOW YELLOW

The Rashtriya Swayamsevak Sangh (RSS), or National Volunteer Corps, India's largest and oldest Hindu nationalist group, was planning to launch a new soft drink called *gau jal* (Sanskrit for cow water). The sacred pee was being mixed with aloe vera, gooseberry, and ayurvedic herbs. "Cow urine offers a cure for around 70 to 80 incurable diseases like diabetes," said spokesman Om Prakash. "All are curable by cow urine." The RSS has campaigned against Pepsi and Coca Cola, which it saw as a corrupting influence and a tool of Western imperialism. *[R] 12 Feb 2009.*

UNORTHODOX TREATMENT

Lin Zongxiu, from China's Sichuan province, was worried about her 25-year-old daughter's (unspecified) psychiatric problems, so she paid a man to behead a 76-year-old drunkard. She then boiled up the head with a duck, and fed the resultant soup to her daughter. We presume the medicine was ineffective. *D.Telegraph, 24 June 2009.*

RELIGIOUS RULINGS

GOAT SPEAKS OUT

According to Ugandan state radio, a goat proclaimed that the AIDS epidemic was a divine punishment for disobeying the Ten Commandments. The goat spoke in a "loud, terrifying voice" to the villagers of Kyabagala, in Mukono district, but died a few hours later. It also predicted that Uganda was on the verge of a great famine. *[AFP] 3 June 1992.*

LITTLE GREEN DEVILS

Aliens are among us and are under Satanic control, said UFO Concern, a predominantly Anglican pressure group founded by Lord Hill-Norton, former Chief of Defence Staff. Gordon Creighton, editor of *Flying Saucer Review* and a Buddhist, agreed. He said: "I believe that the bulk of these phenomena are what is called Satanic." *D.Telegraph, 28 Feb 1997.*

HUMPED BEAUTIES

Sheikh Abdul-Rahman al-Barrak, a leading Wahabi Islamic authority in Saudi Arabia, condemned camel beauty contests as evil, saying those involved should seek repentance. He said that God created camels "for food, drink, riding and work". Camel pageants have become major events as tribes hold ever-larger competitions. Owners spend fortunes primping their charges and winning camels can sell for more than a million riyals (£127,000). *[R] 8 Nov 2007.*

GIRAFFE MILK ALLOWED

Observant Jews may be excited to learn that giraffe milk has been pronounced kosher. Shavuot, the festival of the first fruits, began on 8 June and is traditionally a time for consuming milk products. Vets treating a giraffe at the Ramat Gan safari park near Tel Aviv took a milk sample and found that it clotted in the way required for kosher certification. *D.Telegraph, Independent, 7 June 2008.*

SHAMELESS HUSSIES

Answering questions on the Muslim satellite channel al-Majd, Sheikh Muhammad al-Habadan, an influential Saudi cleric, called on women to wear a full veil, or niqab, that reveals only one eye. Showing both eyes encourages women to use eye make-up to look seductive. However, judging distances will become a problem. *BBC News, 3 Oct 2008.*

MUSLIMS IN DANGER

Malaysia's leading Islamic body, the National Fatwa Council, issued an edict that prohibits Muslims from practising yoga, as its ultimate aim was to become one with a Hindu deity. Earlier, the Council proclaimed that young Muslim women who wore trousers risked becoming sexually active or turning into lesbians. Meanwhile Anjem Choudary, Principal Lecturer at the London School of Shari'ah, said celebrating Christmas "will lead to hellfire". *Guardian, 24 Nov; D.Telegraph, 10 Dec 2008.*

SPREADING THE WORD

Radical preacher Omar Bakri, 50, urged his followers to convert aliens

" Preacher Omar Bakri has urged his followers to convert aliens to Islam "

to Islam. In an online rant from his current home in Lebanon, the Syrian-born firebrand said: "We are obliged as Muslims to make the whole galaxy subservient to almighty Allah." A 'security source' quipped: "Perhaps he could show his people the way – it would give everyone a break if he was beamed up." *Sunday Mercury, 4 Jan 2009.*

CHARLES, PRINCE OF DARKNESS

According to author Tim Cohen, Prince Charles is the Antichrist: his name "calculates to 666 in English and Hebrew"; he is a direct descendant of the "13th Illuminati Bloodline" of the Merovingians (the spawn of the devil); and his Welsh house, Llwyn-y-Wermod, translates as Wormwood Grove, and Wormwood is "the way the world will end". It's all in Cohen's book, *The Antichrist and a Cup of Tea. Wales on Sunday, 5 July 2009.*

SCARY CRITTERS

DEAD GORGEOUS

Zombie mania gripped central Java. Some said the *hantu pocong* – the walking dead – were goat-like creatures or beautiful women. Others said they were white, taller than an average man and exuded a putrid pong. A neighbour, coming to the aid of a screaming woman who had seen a

" Two brothers were fined by a magistrate for keeping a pet ghost "

zombie, attacked it with a machete. It turned out to be a banana tree. *The West Australian, 18 Oct 1997.*

VAMPIRE IN A JAR

Malaysia was abuzz when Hairul Hambali, a bomoh or traditional medicine man, announced on television that he had captured a *langsuir*, a shape-changing vampire, in a cotton tree at Sabak Bernam in Selangor on 21 August 2001. Hambali said it took about an hour to catch the langsuir, which had a small face and resembled a big wad of cotton the size of two tennis balls. He was keeping it in a jar and said it would eventually be thrown into the sea to stop it harassing people. *New Straits Times, 23 Aug; Queensland Times, 25 Aug 2001.*

WINGED CAT FROM HELL

When a large ginger cat with 'wings' turned up in the village of Bukreyevk, near Kursk in central Russia, local people believed it was a messenger of Satan. A journalist from the *Komsomolskaya Pravda* newspaper found that a local drunk had drowned the mutant felid in a sack, but confirmed that it did indeed have 'wings' (probably flaps of skin). *MosNews, 29 July 2004.*

FINED FOR A GHOST

Two brothers were fined by magistrates for keeping a pet ghost. The farmers were told to pay £320 after an exorcist claimed the 'ghost' brought disease to Akshaypur village in West Bengal, India. *Metro, 4 Oct 2005.*

POSSIBLY MISTAKEN

SPACE WARRIOR NABBED

Following complaints of suspicious behaviour, Aaron Millar, 23, was arrested in Victoria, British Columbia, on 5 March 1997. He was dressed in full army fatigues with a helmet and gas mask. He was also wrapped in tinfoil, to protect himself from alien radiation, he explained. He was carrying imitation Molotov cocktails – antifreeze cans filled with water – and two knives. He had cut satellite cables at the *Times-Colonist* newspaper and CHEK Television, possibly in an attempt to halt communication with outer space. *Victoria (BC) Times-Colonist, 7 Mar 1997.*

CULT ICON

Parishioners at 11th-century St Peter-at-Gowts, Lincoln, had unwittingly been praying to Arimanius, god of the dark in the mystery cult of Mithras, thinking it was the Virgin Mary. The effigy, 60ft (18m) up the wall of the tower, was thought to be Anglo-Saxon, "a woman with a funny hair-do", according to archæologist David Stocker, who matched the image to other representations of Arimanius. *D.Telegraph, 14 June 1997.*

EASY PC

John Stevens, 32, a computer programmer from Philadelphia, said his computer showed signs of a virus a week before he got sick – and was convinced he had caught the virus from his machine. His doctor, Dr Mark Fordland, agreed. "He has become forgetful, like something is eating up his memory, his data. He has less and less energy. Even an EEG of his brainwaves keeps changing. The virus could eat him up until his mind is a blank and he's like a vegetable." *Computer Weekly, 26 Mar 1998.*

LOSING HIS MIND

An unidentified man in his late 20s walked into a police station in Ohio with a 9in (23cm) wire protruding from his forehead and asked officers to give him an X-ray to help him find his brain. The man had drilled a 6in (15cm) deep hole in his head with a power drill and had stuck the wire in to try and find the brain. *Salt Lake (UT) Tribune, 18 June 1998.*

NO CHANCE

A 50-year-old woman, taken to hospital with stomach pains, was found to have her vagina fastened with safety pins, and pieces of chicken in her uterus. The woman explained that she had cut up the chicken and put the pieces inside her in the belief that they would grow into a baby. The report said that she was "resting in a special place". *Xit (Åland, Finland), Mar 2003.*

FEARSOME FANS

A majority of South Koreans are apparently convinced that leaving an electric fan turned on in your bedroom overnight can be fatal. Various explanations are given, from the fan's cooling effect resulting in hypothermia to the vacuum created around the victim's face. Korean newspapers report an annual average of 10 fan deaths. Fans are fitted with timer switches as a safety precaution. See Robin Prime's website, www.fandeath.net *Metro, 17 July 2006.*

HEALING PRESIDENT

On 18 January, Yahya Jammeh, 41, the President of Gambia, announced that he could cure asthma on Fridays and Saturdays and HIV/Aids on Mondays and Thursdays. Patients began to queue up at State House in the capital, Banjul. Mr Jammeh, in power since 1994, said he had long had mystic powers but had only recently received a "mandate" to treat large numbers of people. "My method is foolproof," he said. "Within three days the person will be [HIV] negative." Rumour had it the treatment used seven herbs mentioned in the Koran. *Independent, 3 Feb; Scotsman, 21 Feb 2007.*

Chapter 14

DUH!

Musician Frank Zappa once claimed
that stupidity was the basic building
block of the Universe. Our inventory
of idiots – like the man who tried to
commit suicide by crucifying himself –
certainly offers strong evidence
for this proposition.

STUPID IS AS STUPID DOES...

STEELIE OLDIE

A fireman using a metal detector to trace water hydrants covered by tarmac on roads in Bath, Somerset, dug seven holes without finding any hydrants before realising his steel toecaps were activating the device. *D.Telegraph, 25 July 1986.*

POLICE INTELLIGENCE

When police officers were unable to execute a search warrant on a building to which the only entry was a huge steel door, PC Dean Cunnington of Albany Street police station in London borrowed a postman's uniform, put it on, strode up to ther door and knocked hard. "Who is it?" called a voice from within. "It's the police," said Constable Cunnington. *Guardian, 27 Dec 1996.*

MELTDOWN

A Belgian lorry driver, carrying tons of chocolates and trapped by the coldest weather in years, tried unfreezing his fuel tank with a blow-torch. The diesel fuel caught fire and he ended up with a giant chocolate fondue. *[R] 3 Jan 1997.*

BANG THE BOMB

Sappers defused a World War II shell that a villager in Mishenki, Belarus, had been using as an anvil for 50 years to beat nails straight with a hammer. *Dundee Courier, 22 Jan 1998.*

NEIGHBOURHOOD WATCH

Private detectives followed a man from Notton, Yorkshire, for four years in an attempt to prove that an accident had not left him as severely injured as he claimed. They secretly filmed him leading an apparently normal life. Only when the film was sent to William Hood's solicitors did the detective find out that they had been following his neighbour, Peter Arnott, by mistake. Hood won his claim for damages and Arnott was considering suing for invasion of privacy. *D.Telegraph, 11 May 1998.*

TO PROTECT AND SERVE

The inscription on the metal bands used to tag migratory birds in the USA used to bear the address of the Washington Biological Survey, abbreviated to "Wash.Biol.Serv". That was until the agency received a letter from a camper in Arkansas: "Dear Sirs, while camping last week I shot one of your birds. I think it was a crow. I followed the cooking instructions on the leg tag and I want to tell you it was horrible." The bands are now marked: "Fish and Wildlife Service". *New Scientist, 10 Oct 1998.*

TOURIST TWITS

Jeff Hamblin, the chief executive of the British Tourist Authority, recalled some of the odder questions from the time he ran the US office: "When is the next performance of the Piccadilly Circus?", "When is the Edinburgh Festival on in London?" and "Are the Cotswolds open on Sundays?" *Times, 12 Mar 1999.*

CHAMPION DIMWIT

A 32-year-old Austrian who admitted making more than 40,000 obscene telephone calls in Vienna was caught when one of his victims managed to obtain his telephone number. The woman, who had been pestered every day for six months, said she was too busy for an obscene call at that moment but would phone back if he left his number. *Sunday Times, 9 May 1999.*

DOING HIS HEAD IN

William Bartron, 25, of Lehighton, Pennsylvania, accidentally cut off his hand with a power saw, so to take his mind off the pain he shot himself repeatedly in the head with a nail gun. He arrived at the hospital with at least a dozen inch-long nails protruding from his scalp. Surgeons reattached his hand. *[AP] 25 Jan 2001.*

PASSIVE SMOKING

William Hainline from Kentucky was arrested after he turned his entire house into a bong. He put a huge mound of marijuana on a barbecue

" The ad read: 'Professional man, 45, head on a stick, seeks similar woman' "

next to an open window, then placed a fan at the other end of the house, which sucked the smoke into the front room, where his 52nd birthday was taking place. *The Week, 15 Feb 2003.*

OUT DAMNED SPOT!

A man tried to get rid of a paint stain on his trousers by putting a litre of petrol in his washing machine. The resulting explosion wrecked not only the machine, but also the kitchen and two walls in his Moscow flat. *Sun, 14 Oct; Independent on Sunday, 19 Oct 2003.*

HOROSCOPE CHALLENGED

A pensioner from Maramures in Romania lodged a complaint against a TV station, claiming their horoscope was unreliable. The woman said the horoscope repeatedly predicted she would receive a big sum of money, but it never arrived although she waited for three months. Officials advised the broadcasters to include an announcement that the horoscope may not be 100 per cent accurate and that they cannot guarantee the truth of astral predictions. *Ananova, 3 Dec 2003.*

DAYLIGHT SAVING

Judith Hall of Gunnedah, spokeswoman for the ADSC (Abolish Daylight Saving Committee) in New South Wales, told the *Sydney Morning Herald*: "No man has the right to choose the time of the rising and setting of the sun, only God."

A reader suggested that when people insist on moving their clocks forward, God should just move the sunrise forward and thwart them that way. *New Scientist, 13 Dec 2003.*

TWO HANDS NOT ENOUGH

On 16 March, a 23-year-old man from Hartland, Maine, nailed one of his hands to a makeshift cross on his living room floor, having attached a note saying "suicide" to the wood. When he realised that he was unable to nail his other hand to the cross, he called 911. It was unclear whether he was seeking assistance for his injury or to nail his other hand down. He denied having seen *The Passion of the Christ*, but said he had been "seeing pictures of God on the computer". *Bangor (ME) Daily News, 16 Mar 2004.*

BARKING MAD

A woman in Hohhot, capital of the Chinese province of Inner Mongolia, crashed her car while giving her dog a driving lesson. The woman, Ms Li, said her dog "was fond of crouching on the steering wheel and often watched her drive," according to the Xinhua news agency. "She thought she would let the dog 'have a try' while she operated the accelerator and brake. They didn't make it far before crashing into an oncoming car." There were no injuries, although both vehicles were slightly damaged. Ms Li paid for repairs. *[AP] 29 Aug 2006.*

PUZZLING AD

The following advertisement appeared in a Sheffield newspaper in 1999: "Professional man, 45, head on a stick, seeks similar woman". The ad had been transcribed from a phone call. We can only hope that hedonistic professional women got the message. *New Scientist, 11 Aug 2007.*

NO FIXED ADDRESS

Irish police have learnt the truth about a mysterious Polish driver booked for committing more than 50 road offences. Garda officers had been puzzled by Prawo Jazdy, who always produced his documents when apprehended, but with a different address each time. Then in June 2007 one officer twigged that Prawo Jazdy is Polish for "Driver's Licence". About 200,000 Poles moved to Ireland as its economy boomed. *Irish Times, 19 Feb 2009.*

PHANTOM KILLER

German Police thought they were hunting the country's most dangerous woman who murdered six people over 16 years. She was called the "phantom of Heilbronn" after the city where she killed a policewoman. Suspicions were based on identical DNA found at 40 crime scenes across Germany, Austria and France. Doubts were raised when the same DNA appeared on documents belonging to a male asylum seeker who had died in a fire. It turned out that cotton swabs used to gather samples were contaminated with the DNA of medical worker Erika S, 71, before being packed. *Times, 26 Mar; Sun, 15 May 2009.*

DUMB BERLINER

A 76-year-old man blew up his car in Berlin after trying to thaw it out by putting a blow heater under the bonnet. Police said he left the heater on next to the frozen windscreen washer and returned indoors. Shortly afterwards he heard two explosions. *Sunday Mercury, 31 Jan 2010.*

ONE BORN EVERY MINUTE

ALIEN STING

People eavesdropping on police radio broadcasts heard an emergency message about a flying saucer crash in a field at Appleton, Cheshire, and a warning about radioactivity from the burning spaceship. Five people raced to the scene and were promptly arrested by little blue men who charged them with telecommunications offences. *Times, 23 Mar 1993.*

MARTIAN CAPER

Serbian-born Dusco Stuppar, 32, resident in France, duped his childhood friend, postman Christophe H, 37, into giving him 650,000 francs (£62,000) to build an underwater city on Mars. He claimed to belong to a secret group of superior beings that had the necessary technology. The postman believed that Stuppar's evil clone had injected explosives into his back, and would detonate them if he told anyone of the Martian scheme. He had to borrow from his family and bank and the affair came to light when he confessed to a psychiatrist. Stuppar had to repay the money and was jailed for 18 months. *Scotsman, 27 Mar 2001.*

ANT SCAM

Wang Zhendong was sentenced to death for running a scam that netted him £200 million. Wang, from China's Liaoning province, charged £650 for a bag of giant black ants, used to make medical elixirs. Investors were promised returns of up to 60 per cent and around 10,000 suckers signed contracts with his company, the Yilisheng Tianxi Group, but the bags were worth only £13. Police investigated in June 2005, but recovered a mere £650,000. Fifteen other staff members were jailed for up to 10 years. *BBC News, Metro, 15 Feb; Irish Times, 22 Nov 2007.*

WONDERS OF MEDICINE

Brent Eric Finley, 38, of Rayville, Louisiana, was jailed in December 2007 for 51 months for bilking friends and family out of $873,787 by convincing them that his wife Stacey was a CIA agent who could arrange to have their medical problems diagnosed by satellite imaging, and that her "colleagues" would then administer drugs to them as they slept. Stacey had been sent down for 63 months the previous August. *[AP] 6 Dec 2007.*

Chapter 15

WHAT'S IN A NAME?

Louise Bottom marries Mark Butt,
Mike Haddock sells his fish shop
to Edwin Fry, and a man called
Augustus Fantom creates havoc at
the Paris Opera. At least none of them
lives in Fucking, Wank or Vomitville...

LEXILINKS

OUTFOXED

Scotland's Buccleuch Hunt ended in mayhem when the lead hound was killed. It had bounded over a hedge and landed on the car of Rev. Dudley Fox, a retired minister driving home along the Maxton-Kelso road. The other fox – the one being chased – got away. *(Scottish) Sunday Mail, 6 Dec 1992.*

THEY MIGHT HAVE KNOWN

David Pryke, 32, was fined £150 at Enfield Magistrates' Court, north London, for exposing himself to a group of horse riders in Flash Lane. *Times, 15 Feb 1994.*

RAIN STOPS PLAY

A production of *Singing in the Rain*, starring Paul Nicholas and complete with designer puddles, was abandoned on 8 June 1995 when a fault in the sprinkler system poured hundreds of gallons of water into the playhouse. *Edinburgh Eve. News, Liverpool Echo, 8 June 1995.*

WHAT A BUZZ

A beekeeper called in to investigate a low buzzing sound found 10,000 bees in five separate colonies beneath the Darlington home of reporter Beezy Marsh. They could not be removed in safety and had to be exterminated. *D.Mail, 26 July 1996.*

I OF THE STORM

Alfonso Nino, 75, a retired Navy pilot from Nipomo, California, who was listed in the telephone book as Al Nino, had more than 100 calls from people blaming him for the El Niño storms of early 1998. One caller told him he was responsible for his daughter losing her virginity because she was unable to get home after a storm had blocked the road and had spent the night in the car with her boyfriend. *Independent, 3 Mar; D.Telegraph, 4 Mar 1998.*

CROSSING THE FIELD

A middle-aged physiotherapist had every one of her ribs broken when she was trampled by a herd of cows while walking her dog through a field in Bloxham, Oxfordshire. Helen Cowmeadow also suffered a broken collarbone and punctured lung, yet managed to stagger 600 yards (550m) to get help. *D.Mail, 10 April 1998.*

LIVING UP TO YOUR NAME

American businessman Timothy Tipsy flew home a day late after being barred from an earlier flight because he was drunk. Staff at Gatwick had called police after Mr Tipsy, 42, became abusive. *Times, 26 Aug 1998.*

FANTOM OF THE OPERA

A man was arrested in the Paris Opera House after allegedly soaking carpets with a fire hose, causing £2,000 worth of damage. He was a 27-year-old translator from Weston-Super-Mare – called Augustus Fantom. *Western Daily Press, 28 Aug 1999.*

TITLE REALISED

The veteran *Tomorrow's World* reporter Peter Snow was lucky to survive after a light plane in which he was a passenger crashed into trees on Bainbridge Island, off Seattle, in early October 1999. This was the exact location of the best-selling novel by David Guterson, called *Snow Falling On Cedars*. *Guardian, 4+5 Oct 1999.*

BIBLICAL JEST

Jesus appeared before Pontius in January 2000. Jesus Jerusalem, 28, pleaded not guilty in Blackfriars Crown Court in London to two counts of assault. Judge Timothy Pontius ordered him to face trial by jury. *Sunday Mail, 16 Jan 2000.*

WELL NAMED?

The engineer in charge of a British Waterways project to repair holes in the banks of the Grand Union Canal, near Milton Keynes, is Lee King. *Sunday Telegraph, 16 July 2000.*

" 'A medical practitioner advised us to paste her with chicken shit' "

DEVIL'S WORK?

A year after filming *The Omen* (released in 1976), the special effects man crashed his car in Holland. When he came to, his assistant was dead beside him – and the nearest signpost read "Ommen, 66.6 km". *D.Telegraph, 27 Oct 2005.*

I BEE WED

A swarm of 10,000 bees held up a wedding between Emma Busby, 26, and Stephen Pollen, 29, in Cranleigh, Surrey. *Sun, 3 July 2006.*

NAME GAMES

DOG FALLS AT DITTO

A 14-year-old collie-Jack Russell cross called Kyle was rescued on 8 July 2007 after falling 50ft (15m) into a ravine called Dog Falls. Kyle, who is partially blind and deaf, was unharmed despite spending more than four hours in the water at the beauty spot in Glen Affric, near Inverness in the Scottish Highlands. (The spot is called Dog Falls because the water falls in the shape of a dog's leg). *D.Mail, 10 July 2007.*

JACKPOT!

An unnamed punter, believed to be in his 60s, visited the William Hill's in Thirsk, North Yorkshire, on 22 February 2008 and put 50p on eight horses to win in a multiple bet called an accumulator, at combined odds of 2.8 million to one. All eight horses won and the man collected exactly £1 million, William Hill's maximum payout on horseracing, which it said had never been reached in a betting shop before. The first winner was a horse called Isn't That Lucky and the last was one called A Dream Come True. *Sunday Telegraph, 24 Feb 2008.*

JESUS IS BORN

Virgen Maria Huarcaya Palomino, 20, married to a carpenter (Adolfo Jorge Huaman, 24), gave birth to a baby boy in the early hours of Christmas Day at the National Perinatal Institute in Lima, Peru. She named him Jesús Emanuel. She said her grandfather had chosen her unusual name, which means Virgin Mary in English. She had not felt comfortable with it until now. *BBC News, 26 Dec 2008.*

NAME DROPPING

Ji Shi ('Chicken Shit'), a 19-year-old Chinese student, has changed her name to Yingzi. "She had a serious illness when she was one," said her father, Zhu Xiansheng, of Lindong village in Fujian province. "We didn't think she would survive, but a local medical practitioner advised us to paste her with chicken shit while taking medications he prescribed." She made a miraculous recovery and was formally named Ji Shi in tribute to her treatment. *Irish Times, 10 July 2009.*

NOMINATIVE DETERMINISM

SOMETHING FISHY

After 31 years selling fish and chips at the Highworth Fish Shop near Swindon, Wiltshire, Michael Haddock, 64, sold up to Edwin Fry and his son Jamie. *Western Daily Press, 20 Nov 1997.*

MONEY MEN

The new man responsible for handing out lottery money for Camelot is Martin Money, 37. He was about to marry Penny Kippin. And the governor of the English-speaking Caribbean island of San Andres, sacked amid allegations of cronyism, was Maffya Bent. *Sunday Telegraph, 5 Sept; D.Telegraph, 17 Nov 1999.*

HAPPY FAMILIES

Crossing supervisor Alan Rhodes saw the children across the street to Greenhill Primary School, Sheffield, where teacher Linda Bell signalled the start of lessons – with a bell. Reading and writing were taught by Jane Reid and Graham Wright. Heather Tune taught music, with Ian Sharp helping the children with the high notes. IT lessons were given by Sue Smart and Emma Wise. The caretaker, Charles Dyson, vacuumed the floors. *Sunday Express, 23 Nov 2003.*

FITTING NAMES #1

Ben Constable and Audrey Sergeant went to the same school. Ben joined the Northumberland police force and became Constable Constable. Audrey joined the Durham police and eventually became Sergeant Sergeant. The two got married and she outranked him till he got promoted to inspector. *(Melbourne) Herald Sun, 23 May 2008.*

FITTING NAMES #2

Teachers at Frederick Gough School in Scunthorpe included Jan Cook, who taught cookery, Christopher Wood, who taught carpentry, and Barbara Tune, head of music. Mrs Tune's maiden name was Gardener, which didn't suit her: "Every plant I buy dies," she said. *Sun, 27 June 2008.*

FLOCKING TOGETHER

STRICTLY FOR THE BIRDS

A three-bedroomed, riverside house called The Laurels was built in 1911 in Cockermouth, Cumbria, by a builder named Wren. Soon after, two sisters called Wren (no relation) moved in. In 1919, they were replaced by Mary Raven and in July 1920 the cottage was bought by Alfred Rook, who died in 1968. The Martins failed to agree a sale, so Les and Margaret Partridge moved in. Now 76 and widowed, Mrs Partridge has no plans to take flight. Directly behind the house lives a family called Peacock. *D.Telegraph, D.Mail, 14 Mar 2000.*

TELL IT TO THE BIRDS

Gemma Bird, of Fordingbridge, Hampshire, married vet Graham Robins on 27 November 2004. The best man was William Finch, while Stella Rook was a bridesmaid. *Sun, 27 Nov 2004.*

AVIAN RESHUFFLE

James Bird replaced Pam Peacock as the head of the Huntingdonshire branch of the RSPB (Royal Society for the Protection of Birds). Ms Peacock, who had been group leader for 18 years, would continue to serve as a committee member. *Peterborough Eve. Telegraph, 18 Sept 2006.*

YOU MUST BE JOKING!

CRUEL CHRISTENINGS

The following names, all genuine, were culled from the *Daily Telegraph*'s death notices by Rev Arthur Revell: Duane Pipe; Ida Down; Chris Cross; Wyre Walker; Sandy Pitts; and Laurie Loade. *D.Telegraph, 26 April 2000.*

MEMORABLE MOLECULES

Bristol University has a website listing molecules with silly names. Highlights include: Parisite, a mineral; Moronic acid; Cummingtonite; Fukalite: Traumatic acid, a plant hormone; Erotic acid (or vitamin B13); Apatite (a phosphate mineral); Dictite, a clay-like mineral; and Arsole, inspiration for "Studies on the Chemistry of Arsoles" in the *Journal of Organometallic Chemistry. Independent on Sunday, 1 Feb 2004.*

KEEPING THEIR NAME

In 2004, the 150 or so residents of the Austrian village of Fucking voted against changing the name, despite road signs being regularly stolen by Anglophones. Spokesman Siegfried Hoeppl said the name came from Herr Fuck and his family who settled in the area 100 years ago, while the suffix "-ing" meant village or settlement. Locals didn't know the English meaning until Allied soldiers arrived in 1945. Similar votes on a name-change took place in the Austrian towns of Wank am see, Vomitville and Windpassing. *Ananova, 8 June 2004.*

PUNS RULE OK

John Hardie's Chichester plumbing company, All Cisterns Go, won the title of Britain's Best Business Name 2005. The runners-up included car valet firm Rub 'n' Hoods, clothes hire business 20th Century Frox, Indian restaurant Balti Towers, Bangers & Flash Fireworks and a garage called Tyred & Exhausted. *Shropshire Star, 19 Dec 2005.*

NOT WHAT YOU THINK

Be careful when choosing a web address, as running words together can create unwitting ambiguity. Energy giant Powergen in Coventry said it has no connection to the Italian website www.powergenitalia.com. Powergen Italia is actually an Italian battery firm, which was unaware that running its name together in its URL would prove amusing to English speakers. Behind penisland.org was Pen Island, a firm specialising in making pens as corporate gifts. Mole Station Nursery, a garden centre in New South Wales, suggested something more distasteful with the web address molestationnursery.com *Sunday Mercury, 22 June 2003; Metro, 21 Feb 2006.*

CORNISH FANCIES

The Cornwall Record Office has been compiling a list of amusing names for some time. Highlights include Narcissus Backway (1728), Boadicea Basher (1881), Absolom Beaglehole (1841), Honour Bound (d.1783), Philadelphia Bunnyface (d.1722), Fanny Cobbledick (1832), Noah Flood (d.1741), James Jam (1772), Levi Jeans (1797), Ostrich Pockinghorn

" Among the candidates competing for seats in the small Indian state were Billy Kid Sangma and Adolf Lu Hitler Marak "

(1792), Fanny Scum (1805), and Clobery Silly Woolcock (1848). Records also mention Faithful Cock, Abraham Thunderwolff, Edward Evil, Fozzitt Bonds, Charity Chilly, Gentle Fudge, Obedience Ginger and Offspring Gurney. In 1636, Priscilla Skin married Nicholas Bone, while John Mutton and Ann Veale tied the knot in 1791. *Independent on Sunday, 18 Feb 2007.*

MAKING POLITICS FUN

Among the 331 candidates competing for legislative seats on 3 March in Meghalaya, ("Abode of the Clouds"), a small state in northeast India, were: Frankenstein Momin, Billy Kid Sangma, Adolf Lu Hitler Marak, Britainwar Dan, Admiral Sangma, Bombersingh Hynniewta, Laborious Manik Syiem, Hilarius Pohchen, Boldness Nongrum, Clever Marak, and Tony Curtis Lyngdoh. *CNN, 25 Feb 2008.*

NUPTIAL NAMES

A YAWN A MINUTE

Truly Gold married Cary S Boring in September 1994 and took his name, becoming Truly Boring. "I'm not really boring," said Mrs Boring, 24. "I can be the life of any party." *Int. Herald Tribune, 12 Oct 1994.*

WHERE'S WALLY?

Jennifer Pratt (31) who suffered years of ridicule over her name got to change it when she married Tim Burke (37) in Basingstoke, *Hampshire. Sun, 18 Jan 2001.*

STILL BUTT OF GAGS

Louise Bottom, 22, shed her embarrassing name on 9 May when she married Marc Butt, 28, in Cardiff. She reckons life will be more bearable as Mrs Butt. *Sun, 9 May 2001.*

HAPPY FLOWERS

On 21 September, Sarah Lilley, 37, and Michael Rose, 42, of Canterbury, Kent, were married by The Rev Hugh Flowers. Rob Plant was the best man. *Sun, 21 Sept 2004.*

FOND OF NUTS

Sarah Johnson, 56, married third husband Gareth Almond in Wisbech, Cambridgeshire – after divorcing Mark Hazel and Stephen Brazil. *Sun, 30 Jan 2006.*

FOND OF TREES

Emily Chester, 62, of Dunstable, Bedfordshire, wed Simon Beech in September, after previous marriages to Ted Ash and Nigel Oakes. *The People, 14 Sept 2008.*

Chapter 16

WEIRD WORLD

Crude oil gushing from the toilet,
houseplants that burst into flames
and artichokes that explode when
peeled – sometimes the laws of nature
seem to have been temporarily
suspended on our mad planet.

ODD OOZINGS

SHOCKING DRIP

Water started spouting from Guiseppe Galli's walls and electric sockets in Pesaro, Italy. A plumber could find nothing wrong; neither could the fire brigade, who suggested poltergeist trouble. Galli moved out and called a priest. *Sunday Express, 13 Aug 1995.*

SHIRLEY NOT?

Dr Ernesto Moshe Montgomery, clairvoyant and pastor of the Beth Israel Temple in Los Angeles, announced that a picture of Shirley MacLaine, autographed and presented to him by the actress, had been shedding tears. *Denver (CO) Post, 23 May 1997.*

BUBBLING CRUDE

Leila Le Tourneau returned from work as a nurse on 2 February 2004 to find crude oil covering the floor of her house in Longview, East Texas, and gushing out of the sinks, lavatory and bathtub. One theory was that the house was built on an abandoned oil well that was not properly plugged. *Canberra Times, 7 Feb 2004.*

SWEATING GOD

Devotees thronged to a remote shrine in Dolakha, 90 (or 43) miles 145km (or 70km) east of Kathmandu in Nepal, after the stone idol of the god Bhimeshwor, the god of trade, began "sweating". This reportedly happened in 1932 (or 1934) before an earthquake killed thousands of people, and most recently in January (or May) 2001, six months (or a few days) before Crown Prince Dipendra shot dead his father the king and eight other relatives. It happened again in 2006 during street protests that forced King Gyanendra to relinquish direct rule – and in May 2007. *[R] 23 June 2004. BBC News, 21 May; D.Telegraph, 22 May 2007.*

BLEEDING MIRACLE

In March 2007, two portraits of Christ belonging to Eric Nathaniel, a police radio operator in Port Blair, capital of the Andaman Islands in the Indian Ocean, began exuding red fluid. In the subsequent fortnight, thousands of people flocked to Nathaniel's house to see the "bleeding" portraits. *[R] 21 Mar 2007.*

FIERY MYSTERIES

SHIRT COMBUSTION

Alan Fairless heard a bang in his back garden at around 6am on 21 April 1996. He couldn't work out what it was and went back to bed. He later discovered his green and white Lacoste polo shirt, pegged on his washing line, had burned to a crisp, leaving a few bits of green cloth around the shoulders. None of the other items on the line had been affected. Checks with the Bristol Weather Centre showed the weather that night had been fine with no lightning in the area. *Bristol Journal, 24 April; Weekend Telegraph, 25 May 1995.*

FIRE STARTERS

Two Malaysian girls reportedly caused 40 "bizarre fires" in their home in south-western Negeri Sembilan state in September 1996. Sales executive Lee Soon Siong, 44, said: "Objects just burst into flames when my daughters looked at them." He and his wife had to follow the girls – Jean Jean, 10, and Kean Kean, nine – around the house because when they were left alone mattresses, pillows, newspapers, and even a wet towel were destroyed. Doors opened on their own and the main power switch turned itself off 20 to 30 times a day. *Hong Kong Standard, 23 Sept 1996.*

FINALLY SNUFFED

In November 1997 China put out a fire in the Baiyanghe coalfield that had been burning in the north-western province of Xinjiang since spontaneously igniting in 1560, according to the *Sichuan Daily*, which estimated that during that time it had consumed 127 million tons of coal. *[R, AFP] 29 Nov 1997.*

" An Italian
woman was
peeling an
artichoke when
it gave off sparks
and blew up "

CAT O'NINE TALES

When a black cat emerged unscathed from a raging fire in Seme, Nigeria, people were so alarmed that they clubbed it to death. They tried to burn it, using petrol and tyres, but the carcass resisted the flames. It was disembowelled and found to contain charms, a knife, needles and cowrie shells. The remains were given to the police and a woman claiming to be the cat's owner was in protective custody for fear she could be lynched. *Hong Kong Standard, 13 Feb 1999.*

HOT HOUSE PLANTS

Firemen were called to a house in Sundsvall, Sweden, on 6 March 2001 where smoke billowed from one of the rooms. It originated in a flowerpot containing a red pelargonium. The soil appeared to have spontaneously combusted and was 235 degrees C (487 degrees F) – as hot as a baker's oven. Next day, another Sundsvall woman called the fire brigade as her newly potted pelargonium was smoking. *Expressen (Sweden), 8 Mar 2001.*

EXPLODING ARTICHOKE

An Italian woman was peeling an artichoke when it gave off sparks, then a small flame, and then blew up in her hands. Police rushed to her home near Trieste, fearing that it was the work of a terrorist who for 10 years had been planting explosive devices in food products and supermarkets in northern Italy. However, forensic tests showed no trace of explosives, leading police to conclude that it was a natural phenomenon. *Ananova, 26 Feb 2003.*

HOME SWEAT HOME

Maria Fiandaca and her family fled their house in Riesi, Sicily, after the floors became so hot that they started steaming. They blamed a malevolent ghost. Investigators could not immediately find any scientific explanation. *Sun, NY Post, 7 May 2009.*

PREDICTIVE POWERS

SHOW ME THE MONEY!

Colin Roberts, 46, from Newport, South Wales, searched a field near Magor, Monmouthshire, with his metal detector and turned up the odd coin. Then he dreamed that he was in the middle of the field finding a large number of coins. When the dream repeated a few nights later, he took a few hours off from his job as a plumber and returned to the field. He walked to the middle and his detector bleeped. He unearthed 3,778 Roman coins, including 700 from the reign of the "usurping" Emperor Allectus from the late third century. *Times, 11 Dec 1998.*

SCRAPYARD VISION

An SA80 high-powered military rifle was stolen from a dog handler's van inside Episkopi Garrison, a British base in Cyprus. Lesley Eddy, 37, an RAF sergeant's wife who gave psychic consultations, offered her services and had a vision of burned-out buses, dead grass and old cars. A corporal recognised the description of an old compound full of wrecked vehicles from the Turkish invasion of the island in 1974. The rifle, plus night sights and ammo, were found intact under a car. *Sun, 27 Nov 1999.*

DREAM TRANSPLANT

Dorel Vidican, 30, serving three years in a Romanian jail for armed robbery, saved the life of a woman after claiming to have been told in a dream that he was the only person able to help her. Diana Moldovan, 39, would have died without a kidney transplant. Vidican, 30, asked to help after seeing her on TV. Doctors found his tissue was 100 per cent compatible – a one in 16 million chance. President Ion Iliescu then gave Vidican a pardon. *Metro, 28 June; Irish Examiner, 18 July 2002.*

BEEN THERE, SEEN THAT

After a woman told a court in Oslo she was clairvoyant, she was dropped from the jury. She said she already knew what verdict she would reach as she had "seen" the crime enacted through her crystal ball. *Sunday Independent (Ireland), 9 June 2002.*

NO ESCAPE

While away for the weekend, US schoolteacher Charise Hartzol had a dream that foretold her death. Worried, she packed her things and started for home. Halfway there, her car was involved in an accident and her premonition came true. *Independent on Sunday, 1 May 2005.*

UNUSUAL ABILITIES

SQUEEZE

Bank robber Christopher Jeburk, 20, escaped from jail in Appling, Georgia, through a window only 7in (18cm) wide and then scaled a 12ft (3.6m) fence. "It is a puzzle how any human being could have fitted through such a tiny window," said a guard. Perhaps Jeburk was like the flexible Eugene Toombs in the *X-Files. D.Mirror, 26 June 1996.*

BRIGHT SPARKS

A Romanian electrician claimed he could touch live domestic wiring without getting a shock. Constanti Craiu, 51, from Buzau, discovered his gift by accident in 1972 while working on a circuit board. Local media dubbed him the Electric Man. In 2008, in front of journalists, he put two wires into an electric socket and used his hands as conductors to turn on a lamp. Georgi Ivanov, 80, a Bulgarian electrician, demonstrated the same voltage immunity in 1984. *Metro, 22 Jan 2002; North West Eve. Mail, 3 June 2008.*

INFANT PRODIGY

Shraddha Vajapeyee, a three-year-old Indian girl from Janakipur near Lucknow, could recite up to 3,000 sutras (verses) from the *Ashta adhyayi*, a Sanskrit treatise on grammar and linguistics, even though she couldn't read Sanskrit. Her father, Ravi Shankar (no, not that one), said she learnt the entire tome by heart when she was two and a half. She displayed her talent at public functions and was famous across the country. *Irish Examiner, 6 Feb 2003.*

SPEAKING IN TONGUES

Tatti Valo, 23, a woman from the south Russian town of Anapa, claimed to be able to speak 120 languages, according to *Komsomol'skaya Pravda*. Linguists had allegedly identified 16th-century English, Chinese, Persian, Egyptian, Mongolian, Vietnamese, Korean and Swahili. Ms Valo said she remembered them from her past lives. "They just came to me one day 10 years ago in a mathematics class at school," she said. *Ananova, 1 May 2003.*

THROUGH A GLASS DARKLY

Rafael Batyrov, 11, in Russia's Bashkir Republic, claimed the ability to diagnose people's illnesses from their reflection and then cure them. "I discovered my gift about a year ago," he said. "My father was reading an article about a person who could see through people. I told him I could do the same and asked him to sit in front of a mirror, and then I enumerated his illnesses one after the other." He then read a prayer over a can of tap water and cured his father. He was seeing up to 20 people a day and had cured several of his schoolteachers. *Pravda (Russia), 3 Mar 2005.*

INVISIBLE MAN

Ye Xiangting of China's Henan province went to get a new identity card. He sat for the camera but failed to appear in the photograph. The equipment was checked and another photo taken; but still no Ye Xiangting. Then he was photographed with others; the others showed up, but he didn't. There have, apparently, been two similar cases in the past. *Independent on Sunday, 22 Jan 2006.*

PI RECORD

Akira Haraguchi, 60, a Japanese mental health counsellor, set a new record on 4 October 2006 by reciting pi to 100,000 decimal places, a feat of memory that took over 16 hours before a crowd in a suburban Tokyo conference hall. He was allowed 10 minute breaks every two hours, and broke his own record of 83,431, set in 1995. Most of us can only manage three decimal places: 3.141. *Independent, 5 Oct; Shropshire Star, 7 Oct 2006.*

HARUSPICATION

Paul Smokov, 84, a rancher in the US Midwest, makes long-range weather forecasts by consulting pig spleens. The foot-long organs he examined in December 2007 were uniform in thickness, meaning that there would be no drastic changes. "The spleens are 85 per cent correct, according to my figures," he said. As for the weathermen, "those guys aren't any better." *Irish Examiner, 27 Dec 2007.*

THE UNNATURAL WORLD

SUTURE SELF

Doctors in Malawi were mystified by the reappearing sutures that plagued Opani Banda, 14. Removed in hospital on 17 November 1995, they reappeared the following morning. Opani returned to have them removed again, but by mid-afternoon they had reappeared at random on the left side of her body. "This is witchcraft," said orthopædic officer Philip Mayendayenda. The sutures appeared wire-like or nylon in texture.

TUESDAY

" Mr Smokov makes long-range weather forecasts by consulting pig spleens "

Opani was said to have had them for a year, following a family feud. A witchdoctor had failed to get rid of them. *[AFP] 19 Nov 1995.*

IS IT A PLANT?

Staff at the Pot and Plant Centre in Kidnappers Lane, Leckhampton, near Cheltenham, were puzzled by what they found on 27 January 1996. Shoe prints led from the nursery to a pile of clothes (hooded jacket, size 9 men's boots, socks and a PVC flat cap). Beyond the clothing, a set of bare footprints led to a hawthorn bush. Police were stumped. *Western Daily Press, 31 Jan 1996.*

FISH OUT OF WATER

Chen Yiyu, vice-president of the Chinese Academy of Sciences, dis-covered a fish in a water pit near the Number 4 Tazhong Oilfield in the remote Xinjiang Uygur Autonomous Region – an area where aquatic life was believed not to be viable. The pit had been carved out with bulldoz-ers during highway construction, and had eventually filled with slightly saline ground water, to which the black, freshwater fish had adapted. Chen had ruled out the possibility that the fish was brought to the desert by people working there. *Victoria (BC) Times-Colonist, 19 July 1998.*

FIG TREE ANGEL

In July 2000, people reported seeing an angel – a white-robed, glowing figure – sitting in the branches of a 100-year-old fig tree in Jerusalem. Citing "security concerns", the Israelis erected a protective fence and stationed soldiers to mount guard round the tree. *(Scottish) Sunday Mail, 5 Nov 2000.*

ORCHARD FISHING

An orchard owner landed a record-breaking trout without baiting a hook. Philip Greenhow found the 10lb (4.5kg) fish lying on the ground among the trees. It was 2lb (0.9kg) heavier than the biggest recorded catch from the nearby River Otter in Devon. The retired surveyor believed record floods had swept the trout into his orchard. *Metro, 9 Mar 2001.*

LETHAL LIKENESS

A portrait of University College Hospital benefactor Marcus Beck disappeared recently during refurbishment. The picture of Beck, who wrote about septicæmia arising from pus-filled sores and died prematurely in 1893, had acquired a killer reputation. Actor Damian Lewis fell asleep under the newly-hung portrait, woke up covered with suppurating abscesses, and died in agony. He was the first of so many victims that the night sister was charged with drawing curtains (or possibly wooden shutters) over it every night... *Times, 5+9+10+13 Jan 2001.*

CAN OF WORMS

As Sue Crane from Cardiff began to open a tin of Whiskas to feed her cats, it exploded and covered her face with maggots and flies. "It was like something out a horror movie," she said. *Irish Independent, 24 May 2003.*

DAMNED HOLES

Villagers in Chongqing, south-west China, have been plagued for the last 32 years by small holes appearing in clothes and other fabrics. Some residents have fled, fearing the place is cursed. A medium, called in to exorcise the spirits, also cleared off when holes appeared in his clothes. Officials say the holes, which only occur while clothes are not being worn, result from movements in the Earth's magnetic field. So that's all right then. *Independent on Sunday, 17 Oct 2004.*

AERIAL CITY

Thousands of people in the Chinese port of Penglai in Shandong province witnessed a prolonged mirage of "high clarity" that lasted for more than four hours. Mists rising on the shore created an image of a city with high-rise buildings, broad streets, and large crowds. Such mirages had been seen before and had earned the city a reputation as a dwelling place for the gods. *[UPS] Rocky Mountain News (Denver), 15 May 2006.*

STAFFORD WEREWOLF

West Midlands Ghost Club was contacted by a postman and a scout leader, both of whom claimed separate sightings of a "hairy wolf-type creature" around the German War Cemetery, just off Camp Road, between Stafford and Cannock. At first, the postman thought it was a large dog. But when he got closer, the creature got on its hind legs and ran away. The scout leader said it was 6-7ft (1.8-2m) tall. There have been many mysterious encounters over Cannock Chase, including sightings of a 'Bigfoot' type creature. *Stafford Post, 26 April 2007.*

PHANTOM FISH OIL?

During the morning of 26 April 2007, a strong and musty smell, reminiscent of a rubbish tip or herring oil factory, settled on the Norwegian town of Bergen and its surroundings. There had been several herring-oil factories surrounding Bergen, but they had been long closed down. The source of the smell was undetermined. *Metro (Malmö, Sweden), 27 April 2007.*

MOTH-WATERING

Richard Bach from Dorchester, Dorset, sliced open a red pepper grown in Spain and found a live moth inside. *D.Star, 11 Jan 2008.*

" A conman masquerading as a priest hypnotised Italian shop-keepers into giving him their cash "

SPELLBOUND

HYPNOHEIST

A robber hypnotised a woman and stole her salary as she withdrew it from an Indian bank. Ishrat Ali Lalljee, 37, was in a Bank of India branch in Mumbai when a man mumbled something in her ear. The 37-year-old said she felt helpless and the man escaped with the equivalent of £89. She said: "For the next 30 seconds I was spellbound. By the time I got my bearings it was too late." *Times of India, 27 Feb 2001.*

SPECIAL POWERS

A conman masquerading as a priest who hypnotised Italian shopkeep-ers into handing over cash and jewellery was arrested in March 2004. He was seen on CCTV going into a jewellers and waving his fingers towards his victim, who then opened the till and gave him cash. *Scotsman, 31 Mar 2004.*

FORTEAN TIMES WOULD LIKE TO THANK:
The many readers who, over the years, have sent in the newspaper clippings or
Internet links from which the stories in this volume have been compiled.

GET INVOLVED – BECOME A FORTEAN TIMES CLIPSTER!
Regular clipsters have provided the lifeblood of **Fortean Times** since it began
in 1973. One of the delights for the editors is receiving packets of clips from
Borneo or Brazil, Saudi Arabia or Siberia. We invite you to join in the fun and send
in anything weird, from trade journals, local newspapers, extracts from obscure
tomes, or library newspaper archives.

To minimise the time spent on preparing clippings for a Fort Sort, we ask
that you cut them out and not fold them too small. Mark each clip (on the front,
where possible) with the source, date and your name, so that we can credit you
in the listing when we use the material. For UK local and overseas clips, please
give the town of publication. For foreign language clips, we appreciate brief
translations. To avoid confusion over day and month, please write the date in this
form: 10 May 2010. If you send photocopies, copy on one side of the paper only.

Mail to: **Fortean Times, PO Box 2409, London NW5 4NP, UK**
E-mail: **sieveking@forteantimes.com**
or post on the FT website at **www.forteantimes.co.uk,**
where there is a contributor's guide.